VOLUME 2

The Actual Doctrine of King Jesus

Ronald F. Peters

Suite 300 - 990 Fort St
Victoria, BC, V8V 3K2
Canada

www.friesenpress.com

Copyright © 2018 by Ronald F. Peters
First Edition — 2018

All rights reserved.

No part of this publication may be reproduced in any form, or by any means, electronic or mechanical, including photocopying, recording, or any information browsing, storage, or retrieval system, without permission in writing from FriesenPress.

ISBN
978-1-5255-2084-6 (Hardcover)
978-1-5255-2085-3 (Paperback)
978-1-5255-2086-0 (eBook)

1. RELIGION, CHRISTIAN EDUCATION, ADULT

Distributed to the trade by The Ingram Book Company

Preface

It is the intention of this report

to reveal the thinking,
reaction,
character,
and love of our great God,
and to establish within the reader
a firm relationship
with our Saviour,
His Majesty "King Jesus".

There is nothing new in this book.
It is only a collection of observations,
written in a "question and answer" format,
to be both educational and entertaining
for the reader.

God says in: Revelation 22: 19

And
if any man shall take away
from the words of the book
of this prophecy,
God shall take away his part
out of the "book of life"
and out of the "holy city",
and from the things
which are written
in this book.

Please note that all references are taken from the "King James Version" of the Holy Bible.

Authors Forward

This book has a collection of Christian premises,
taken directly from God's Holy Bible,
which may belie the catechism's,
creed's and doctrinal foundations,
of some of the "Christian Denominations".
The Bible was never meant to be
of private interpretation,
but rather to be known as the infallible word of God :
who does not vary, and he is not the author of confusion.

As an example of these doctrinal differences,
we can look at water baptism,
which is just one of the chapters included in this volume.

Every denomination has it's own version of
"Water Baptism".
Many believe an infant
should be sprinkled with water, to join the church.
Many believe it is an outward proclamation
of what is happening internally .
Martin Luther recommended the baptism
of both infants and adults as a means of grace.
John Calvin thought infant baptism
was similar in theology to infant circumcision .

Typically church membership
is a matter of receiving Jesus
as your Saviour and Lord,
and experiencing "believer Baptism"
as an act of obedience,
symbolizing the believers entire faith.

The apostles wrote the "New Testament" in Greek and some Aramaic.
The "Old Testament" had been written in Hebrew.
After Christ's death and resurrection,
the early Christians
suffered horrible persecution and had to go into hiding.

The records are not complete,
but some of the approximate statistics include:

66AD	-	50,000 Christian Jews killed at Alexandria, Egypt.
		60,000 Christian Jews killed elsewhere
70AD	-	600,000 Christian Jews killed in Judea also 10,000 crucified, and another 90,000 became slaves
81AD	-	40,000 killed in Rome
303AD	-	15,000 killed in Asia Minor
	-	140,000 killed in Egypt
284- 305	-	500,000 executed under Caesar Galerius in Rome

The "Edict of Milan" in 313 AD
by the Roman Emperors
"Constantine the Great" and "Emperor Licinius"
legalized Christianity.
Consequently, many of the original manuscripts that survived,
which had been hidden in jars in catacombs and caves,
were now safe again to be studied.

From 382 to 404 Saint Jerome made Latin translations
which ended with a Latin version called the "Vulgate".
By 600 AD only Latin transcripts of the Bible
were allowed for scripture,
and church dogma demanded
that only a priest should read the Bible.

Around 1384 AD, John Wycliffe, an Oxford professor,
translated some of the Bible
into English from the Latin Vulgate.

John Hus, who promoted these translations,
was subsequently burnt at the stake in 1415.
Oddly enough, the Roman Church
used Wycliffe's translations, to kindle that fire.

In 1490, Thomas Linacre, also an Oxford professor,
and personal physician to King Henry the 8th
learned Greek, and discovered
that the Latin Vulgate was so inaccurate,
that it had not even preserved
the message of the gospels.

In 1514 the first New Testament printed in Greek
was by Cardinal Francisco Jimenez de Cisneros
as part of the "Complutensian Polyglot".

In 1516 Erasmus published his first New Testament in Greek.
In 1519 Erasmus translated his second edition
of the Greek New Testament
known as the "Textus Receptus"
Erasmus also published a revised version of the
Latin New Testament
called the "Novum Testamentum Omne".
In 1522 Erasmus published
the "Complutensian Polyglot Bible"
from both Hebrew and Greek manuscripts.

Around 1522, Martin Luther made a German translation
from the Textus Receptus of the New Testament.
In 1546 - with the help of six other exceptional German scholars,
Martin Luther published his final version
of the whole Bible.

In 1526 William Tyndale translated and printed
a great New Testament translation in English,
however, anyone caught in mere possession of it,
was burned at the stake.

In 1536 Tyndale himself was burned at the stake.

In 1535 Myles Coverdale printed the complete
Bible in English.

In 1537 John Rogers printed
the second complete English Bible.

In Between 1535 and 1541 King Henry VIII
commissioned Thomas Cramer, the ArchBishop,
who hired Myles Coverdale,
to print seven copies, called the "Great Bible".

In 1555 Queen Mary,
the daughter of King Henry the 8th,
(they called her bloody Mary)
had both John Rogers and Thomas Cramer
burned at the stake.
Queen Mary went on to burn hundreds of reformers,
for the crime of being a Protestant.
Queen Mary died of Ovarian Cancer in 1558.

There were other translations,
but finally in 1611,
there were 47 brilliant scholars chosen,
whom King James commissioned ,
to translate the complete Holy Bible,
which became their famous "King James Version".
About seventy percent of its wording
was borrowed from William Tyndales vivid translation.

The translators were placed into six groups.
The procedure was to assign each translator
a portion of scripture, and then present his work
to the others in his group for approval.
Each book was then sent to the five other groups
for review and criticism.
With this procedure,
each book was scrutinized by every member.
A committee of twelve, two from each team,
made a final review.

King James authorized this " King James Version"
and it also became known as the "Authorized Version".

That authorization looked like this:

The
Holy Bible
containing the
Old and New Testaments

Translated out of the original tongues
and with the former translations
diligently compared and revised
by his Majesty's special command
Appointed to be read in churches

Ronald F. Peters Questions

After the translations were done,
when the early scholars
eventually began to study water baptism,
there were many opinions.

It started with Puritans,
and eventually many denominations were formed,
to follow their own beliefs.

Did God leave it all open to interpretation ?
How could "Water Baptism" become that confusing ?

Should we now condemn the various denominations,
who have not been teaching exactly
what is written in the Holy Bible ?
God forbid .

Each family has followed the beliefs of their heritage,
in good faith, that "truth" was taught to them .
Learning more, is merely what God teaches us to do.
Learning more, is what Christianity is all about.
We are instructed to "study"
to show ourselves approved unto God.

Should any blame be put on our current Theologians ?
God Forbid.
Each seminary,
that instructs their student pastors and teachers ,
can only teach the basic doctrines
of that denomination.
They are actually taught,
that the other denominations
are all on a lower level of doctrine,
and being misguided,
have therefore yet
a considerable way to go ,

to reach their proper and superior level of Christian Doctrine .

There is much information in the Holy Bible
about the purpose of water baptism.

His Majesty, King Jesus said,
"for thus it becometh us, to fulfil all righteousness".
(not just some, all righteousness.) St. Matthew 3:15

Some theologians refer to the thief on the cross,
who wasn't baptized,
but was promised to be in Paradise.
Christ Jesus had not died yet,
and our new covenant was not yet confirmed.
The thief was permitted under Jewish law,
under Abrahams covenant,
to be reprieved by the high priest,
who Jesus was,
after the order of Melchizedek.
He also spoke of the soldiers
who nailed him to the cross,
and said,
"Father, forgive them;
for they
know not what they do".

Table of Contents

Preface vii

Authors Forward ix

Chapter 1 1
    Blinded the Minds

Chapter 2 16
    Who is Jesus ?

Chapter 3 30
    How to study

Chapter 4 39
    Repentance

Chapter 5 52
    Of faith toward God

Chapter 6 66
    The Doctrine of Water Baptism

Chapter 7 95
    The Doctrine of the
    Baptism of the Holy Spirit

Chapter 8 117
    The "laying on of hands"

Chapter 9 129
    The resurrection from the Dead

Chapter 10 145
    Eternal Judgment
    My Friend

Chapter 11 160
    "New Testament" sins

Chapter 12 178
    Idols and Images

Chapter 13 193
    How to stop sinning

Chapter 14 200
    God's gift of Grace

Chapter 15 207
    Darkness and Light

Chapter 16 215
    The Covenants

Chapter 17 231
    The priesthood of Jesus Christ

Chapter 18 248
    King Jesus' final instruction

Chapter 19 259
    God has never been Democratic

Chapter 20 280
    Christians and Politics

Chapter 1.

Blinded the Minds

The Doctrine of Christ
Ronald F. Peters

Question: Is the Bible really as confusing as it looks ?

God says in: 1 Corinthians 14 : 33

> For God is not the author of confusion,
> but
> of peace,
> as in all churches of the saints.

Question: Then why do Christians
seem to understand the Bible ,
and everyone else is confused about it ?

God says in: 2 Corinthians 4 : 3

> But
> if our gospel be hid,
> it is hid to them that are lost:
>
> in whom the god of this world (age)
> hath blinded the minds
> of them which believe not,
>
> lest the light of the glorious gospel of Christ,
> who is the image of God,
> should shine unto them.

Question: What upset God, so that the lost have the Holy Bible hid from them?

God says in: Isaiah 5: 11 – 12

> Woe unto them that rise up early in the morning,
> that they may follow strong drink;
> that continue until night ,
> till wine inflame them !
> and the harp, and the viol,
> the tabret,
> and pipe, and wine are in their feasts:
> but
> they regard not the work of the Lord,
> neither consider the operation of his hands.

Question: Was that all that upset God ?

God says in: Isaiah 5: 20 – 24

> Woe unto them that
> call evil good,
> and good evil;
> that put darkness for light,
> and light for darkness;
> that put bitter for sweet,
> and sweet for bitter!
>
> Woe unto them that are wise in their own eyes,
> and prudent in their own sight!
> Woe unto them that are mighty to drink wine,
> and men of strength to mingle strong drink:
> which justify the wicked for reward,
> and take away the righteousness of the righteous,
> from him!
>
> Therefore
> as fire devoureth the stubble,
> and the flame consumeth the chaff,
> so their root shall be as rottenness,
> and
> their blossom shall go up as dust:
> because they have cast away the law
> of the Lord of hosts,
> and despised the word
> of the Holy One of Israel.

Question: What did God tell his prophet Isaiah to do then?

God says in: Isaiah 6: 9 – 10

    And he said,
    Go,
    and tell this people,
    hear ye indeed,
    but
    understand not;
    and
    see ye indeed
    but
    perceive not.

    Make the heart of this people fat,
    and make their eyes heavy,
    and shut their eyes;

    lest they see with their eyes,
    and hear with their ears
    and understand with their heart,
    and convert,
    and be healed.

Question: Did God really mean that people wouldn't be able to understand Gods word?

God says in: Ephesians 4: 17 – 18

This I say therefore,
And testify in the Lord,
That ye henceforth
walk not as other Gentiles walk,
in the vanity of their mind,
having the understanding darkened,

being alienated from the life of God
through the ignorance that is in them,
because of the blindness of their heart:
who being past feeling
have given themselves over to lasciviousness
to work all uncleaness
with greediness.

Question: Did God close their eyes to the whole Bible and did God ever decide to open their eyes again?

God says in: 2 Corinthians 3: 12 - 16

> Seeing then that we have such hope,
> we use great plainness of speech:
> and not as Moses,
> which put a veil over his face,
> that the children of Israel
> could not stedfastly look
> to the end of that which is abolished:
> but
> their minds were blinded:
>
> for
> until this day
> remaineth the same veil untaken away
> in the reading
> of the old testament;
> which veil is done away in Christ.
>
> But
> even unto this day
> when Moses is read,
> the veil is upon their heart.
>
> Nevertheless
> when it shall turn to the Lord,
> the veil shall be taken away.

Question: Is this why the Bible doesn't make much sense to the non Christians?

God says in: 1 Corinthians 1: 18

> For
> the preaching of the cross
> is to them that perish
> foolishness;
> but
> unto us which are saved
> it is the power of God.

Question: So if a person can only get Bible understanding by turning to the Lord, how can anyone turn to the Lord and understand it?

God says in: 1 Corinthians 1: 21

> For
> after that
> in the wisdom of God
> the world
> by wisdom
> knew not God,
> it pleased God
> by the foolishness of preaching
> to save them that believe.

Question: How exactly then, do people get to believe?

God says in: Romans 10: 13 - 21

For
whosoever shall call upon the name
of the Lord
shall be saved.
How then shall they call on him
in whom they have not believed?
and
how shall they believe in him
of whom they have not heard ?
and
how shall they hear without a preacher?
and
how shall they preach, except they be sent?
as it is written,
How beautiful are the feet of them
that preach the gospel of peace,
and
bring good tidings of good things!
But they have not all obeyed the gospel.

For
Esaias saith,
Lord, who hath believed our report?
So then
faith cometh by hearing,
and hearing,
by the word of God.
But I say,
have they not heard?
Yes verily,
their sound went into all the earth,
and their words unto the ends of the world.

But I say,
did not Israel know?
First Moses saith,
I will provoke you to jealousy
by them that are no people,
and
by a foolish nation
I will anger you.

But
Esaias is very bold,
and saith,
I was found of them that sought me not;
I was made manifest
unto them that asked not after me.
But
to Israel He saith ,
all day long
I have stretched forth my hands
unto a disobedient and gainsaying people.

Question: What does God want preachers to preach ,
and what are people supposed to do,
to get saved ,
so that they can then,
understand Gods Bible ?

God says in: Romans 10 : 8 - 10

But
what saith it ?
The word is nigh thee,
even in thy mouth,
and in thy heart:
that is,
the word of faith,
which we preach;

That if thou shalt confess with thy mouth
the Lord Jesus,
and
shalt believe in thine heart
that God hath raised Him from the dead,
thou shalt be saved.
For
with the heart man believeth unto righteousness;
and
with the mouth confession is made unto salvation.
For
the scripture saith,
whosoever believeth on Him shall not be ashamed.

Question: How does Lord Jesus react to this?

God says in: St. Luke 10 : 21

> In that hour Jesus rejoiced in spirit,
> and said,
> I thank thee,
> O Father,
> Lord of heaven and earth,
> that thou hast hid these things
> from the wise and the prudent,
> and hast revealed them unto babes:
> even so ,
> Father;
> for so it seemed good in thy sight.

Question: Did God really write the Bible
and if so, what is the purpose of the Bible

God says in: 2 Timothy 3 : 16 - 17

> All scripture is given by inspiration of God,
> and is profitable
> for doctrine,
> for reproof,
> for correction,
> for instruction in righteousness :
> that
> the man of God may be perfect,
> thoroughly furnished unto all good works.

Question: So how then did God inspire these men that wrote the Bible ?

God says in: Proverbs 8 : 8 – 11

All the words of my mouth are in righteousness;
there is nothing froward or perverse in them.
They are all plain to him that understandeth,
and right to him that findeth knowledge.
Receive my instruction,
and not silver;
and knowledge rather than choice gold.
For wisdom is better than rubies;
and all things that may be desired
are not to be compared to it.

Question: How exactly did the men in the Holy Bible receive the information that they wrote down ?

God says in: 2 Peter 1: 20

Knowing this first ,
that no prophecy of the scripture
is of any private interpretation .
For the prophecy came not in old time
by the will of man:
but holy men of God
spake as they were moved
by the Holy Ghost.

Question: When did God decide to start the Bible and why is the Bible called the Holy Bible?

God says in: St. John 1 : 1 – 3

In the beginning was the Word
and the word was with God,
and the Word was God.

The same was in the beginning with God.
All things were made by him;
and without him ,
was not anything made that was made.

Question: Is the Holy Bible actually God?

God says in: St. John 1 : 14

And the Word was made flesh,
and dwelt among us,
(and we beheld his glory,
the glory of the only begotten of the Father,)
full of grace and truth.

Question: So, if the Word is actually our Lord - King Jesus, when we read the Bible ,
is it actually King Jesus speaking to us on paper ?

God says in: Hebrews 4 : 12 – 14

> For the word of God
> is quick
> and powerful,
> and sharper than any two edged sword,
> piercing even to the dividing asunder of soul and spirit,
> and of the joints and marrow,
> and is a discerner of the thoughts
> and intents of the heart.
>
> Neither is there any creature that is not manifest in his sight:
> But all things are naked and open
> unto the eyes of him with whom we have to do.
>
> Seeing then
> that we have a great high priest,
> that is passed into the heavens,
> Jesus the Son of God,
> let us hold fast our profession.

Chapter 2

Who is Jesus?

The Doctrine of Christ
Ronald F. Peters

Question: How far back does Jesus go in history ?

God says in: St. John 1 : 1 – 3

In the beginning
was the Word ,
and " the Word was with God " ,
and the Word was God.
The same was in the beginning with God .
" All things were made by him " :
and without him was not anything made
that was made .

Question: Was the " Word " that was with God in the beginning , and making everything , really Jesus Christ ?

God says in: St John 1 : 10 - 14

He was in the world,
" and the world was made by him ",
and the world knew him not .
He came unto his own ,
and his own received him not .

But as many as received him ,
to them gave he power
to become the sons of God,
even to them that believe on his name :

Which were born ,
not of blood,
nor of the will of the flesh,
not of the will of man,
but of God .

And
the word was made flesh,
and dwelt among us ,
(and we beheld his glory,
the glory as of
the only begotten of the Father) ,
full of grace and truth .

Question: If the Word made everything ,
and was made flesh ,
and is the only begotten of the Father ,
then do we see him somewhere
in the creation story ?

God says in: Genesis 1 : 26

And God said,
let " us " make man in " our " image :
and let them have dominion

over the fish of the sea,
and
over the foul of the air ,
and
over the cattle ,
and
over all the earth ,
and
over every creeping thing
that creepeth upon the earth .

Question: But does that " us " refer to Jesus and God ?

God says in: Genesis 2 : 4

These are the generations of the heavens and of the earth
when they were created,
in the day that the " Lord God"
made the earth and the heavens.

Question: When it says " Lord God " is that Lord for Jesus and God for God or is Jesus also God ?

God says in: St Mark 12 : 29

And Jesus answered him
the first of the commandments is ,
Hear,
O Israel ;
" The Lord our God
is one Lord " :

Question: Does that mean that
God the Father is also
Lord Jesus Christ - the Son ?

God says in: St John 17 : 21 - 24

That they all may be one ;
as thou, Father ,
art in me ,
and I in thee,
that they also may be one in us:
that the world may believe
that thou hast sent me .
And the glory which thou gavest me
I have given them ;
that they may be one ,
even as we are one :

I in them,
and thou in me ,
that they may be made perfect in one ;
and that the world may know
that thou hast sent me ,
and hast loved them ,
as thou hast loved me.
Father, I will that they also ,
whom thou hast given me ,
be with me where I am ;
that they may behold my glory,
which thou hast given me:
for thou lovest me
before the foundation of the world.

Question: How can this be ,
that Jesus
and the Father
are one ?

God says in: St John 14 : 6 - 11

Jesus saith unto him ,
I am the way ,
the truth ,
and the life:
no man cometh unto the Father ,
but by me .
If ye had known me,
ye should have know my Father also :
and from henceforth ye know him,
and have seen him .
Philip saith unto him,
Lord ,
shew us the Father
and it sufficeth us .

Jesus saith unto him,
have I been so long time with you ,
and yet hast thou not known me, Philip ?

He that hath seen me
hath seen the Father ;
and how sayest thou then ,
shew us the father ?

Believest thou not
that I am in the Father ,
and the Father in me ?

The words that I speak unto you
I speak not of myself:

but the Father that dwelleth in me,
he doeth the works .
Believe me that I am in the Father ,
and the father in me ,
or else believe me for the very works' sake .

Question: How does the Holy Spirit fit in ,
if Jesus is also the Father God ?

God says in: St John 14 : 16 - 18

And I will pray the Father ,
and he shall give you another Comforter,
that he may abide with you forever;
even the "Spirit of truth" ;
whom the world cannot receive ,
because it seeth him not,
neither knoweth him :

but ye know him :
for he dwelleth with you ,
and shall be in you .
I will not leave you comfortless :
I will come to you .

Question: Does that mean that
Jesus is also the Holy Spirit ?

God says in: St John 14 : 26 – 28

But the Comforter ,
which is the Holy Ghost ,
whom the Father will send
in my name ,
he shall teach you all things,
and bring all things to your remembrance,
whatsoever I have said unto you.
Peace I leave with you ,
my peace I give unto you:
not as the world giveth ,
give I unto you.
Let not your heart be troubled ,
neither let it be afraid .
Ye have heard
how I said unto you ,
I go away ,
and come again unto you .
If ye loved me ,
ye would rejoice ,
because I said I go unto the Father :
for my Father is greater than I .

Question: If Jesus is the Father
then the name of the Father is Jesus .
And if Jesus is the Comforter
then the name of the Holy Ghost is Jesus
Is it true then ,
that Jesus had to leave planet earth
to come back to us
as the Holy Spirit ?

God says in: St John 16 : 7

Nevertheless I tell you the truth ;
it is expedient for you
that I go away :

for if I go not away ,
the Comforter will not come unto you:
but if I depart,
I will send him unto you .

Question: So, what does King Jesus the comforter, actually look like ?

God says in: Colossians 1: 15 – 19

Who is the image of the invisible God,
the first born of every creature:
For by him were all things created,
that are in heaven,
and that are in earth,

visible
and invisible ,
whether they be thrones,
or dominions,
or principalities,
or powers:

all things were created by him,
and for him:
And he is before all things,
and by him all things consist.

And he is the head of the body,
the church,
who is the beginning,
the firstborn from the dead;
that in all things he might have the preeminence.

For it pleased the Father
that in him should all fullness dwell.

Question: Why does he refer to invisible things ?

God says in: Romans 1 : 18 – 21

> For the wrath of God
> is revealed from heaven
> against all ungodliness
> and unrighteousness of men,
> who hold the truth in unrighteousness;
>
> Because that which may be known of God
> is manifest in them;
> for God hath showed it unto them.
>
> For the invisible things of him
> from the creation of the world
> are clearly seen,
>
> being understood by the things that are made,
> even his eternal power
> and Godhead,
> so that they are without excuse:
>
> Because that ,
> when they knew God,
> they glorified him not as God,
> neither were thankful;
>
> but became vain in their imaginations,
> and their foolish heart was darkened.

Question: Is King Jesus actually invisible ?

God says in: 1 Timothy 1 : 17

> Now unto the King eternal,
> immortal ,
> invisible,
> the only wise God,
> be honour
> and glory
> for ever and ever. Amen.

Chapter 3

How to study

The Doctrine of Christ
Ronald F. Peters

Question: Exactly how does God want us to study the Holy Bible ?

God says in: Isaiah 28 : 10

For
precept must be upon precept,
(in the Hebrew it is "hath been upon")
precept upon precept ;
line upon line,
line upon line;
here a little,
and there a little:

Authors Note: Throughout the entire Bible
God has chosen to teach us
thoroughly and professionally.
If you were to take a communication course
you would find, that people only hear
about twenty-five percent of what you say.
Therefore if you repeat an item ,
they have a fifty percent chance of understanding.
That is why the same commercials on TV
are thrown at us so many times , until we get it.

Whenever King Jesus
had something really important to say ,
He would say things like
" Hearken unto me everyone of you, and understand :"
or "Verily, verily, I say unto you ".

Sometimes he says " wherefore" or "therefore "
which immediately signals to us to go back
and read the previous statement,
because it is the premise or reason
on which the next statement is made.

Throughout the Bible , whenever you see the word " if "
you can immediately conclude that it is an equation.
If you do this, you will get this.
The Bible is written in intentional sequence.
Therefore study the whole chapter,
don't just grab a verse.
To confirm a thought,
the intention is written in more than one place.

Question: Whom did God say he would
teach knowledge ?

God says in: Isaiah 28 : 9

Whom shall he teach knowledge ?
and
whom shall he make to understand doctrine ?
them that are weaned from the milk,
and are drawn from the breasts.

Question: What did God mean by
"weaned from the milk ?"

God says in: Hebrews 5 : 12 - 13

For
when for the time (since you became Christians)
ye ought to be teachers,
ye have need that one teach you again
which be the first principles of the oracles of God;
and
are become such as have need of milk,
and
not of strong meat.

Authors Note: What is the first principal of the oracles of God?
God has always intended that
whatever he is teaching us ,
we are preparing ourselves to teach others.
Eventually we are to disciple others
and teach what we have learned so far.
There will never come a time,
when we know it all.
The more you learn ,
the more you find out how little you know.

The principle he is talking about ,
is, "the fastest way to learn, is to start teaching".
It is always the teacher, who learns the most.

Question: What does God say is the difference between milk and strong meat ?

God says in: Hebrews 5 : 14
But strong meat belongeth to them
that are of full age,
even those
who by reason of use
have their senses exercised to discern
both good and evil.

Question: But what does God really mean by "have need of milk ? "

God says in: Hebrews 5 : 13

For everyone that useth milk
is unskillful in the word of righteousness:
for he is a babe.

Question: What is Gods definition of milk ?

God says in: Hebrews 6 : 1 – 2
Therefore
leaving the principles
of the doctrine of Christ (the six principles being the milk)
let us go on to perfection; (let us go on to meat things now)
not laying again (not teaching milk things again)
the foundation of :

1. " **repentance** " from dead works
2. and of " **faith toward God** "
3. of the " **doctrine of baptisms** ",
4. and of " **laying on of hands** ",
5. and of " **resurrection of the dead** ",
6. and of " **eternal judgment** ".

Question: What did God mean back there
in Hebrews 5 : 12 when He said
"when for the time you ought to be teachers,
ye have need that one teach you again",
which be the first principles of the oracles of God ?

God says in: St. Matthew 5 : 18 – 19

Till heaven and earth pass,
one jot or one tittle
shall in no wise pass from the law,
till all be fulfilled
Whosoever therefore shall break
one of these least commandments,
and shall teach men so ,
he shall be called the least
in the kingdom of heaven:
but
whosoever shall " do "
and " teach them ",
the same shall be called great
in the Kingdom of Heaven

Question: What really happens to us
when we aggressively study the word of God ?

God says in: Psalms 119 : 11

Thy word have I hid in my heart,
that I might not sin against thee.

Question: Since the Bible is such a large book , what does God really expect us to study ?

God says in: Ephesians 6: 10 - 17

Finally,
my brethren,
be strong in the Lord,
and in the power of his might.
Put on the whole armour of God,
that ye may be able to stand
against the wiles of the devil.
For we wrestle not against flesh and blood,
but against principalities,
against powers
against the rulers of the darkness of this world,
against spiritual wickedness in high places.
Wherefore
take unto you the whole armour of God,
that ye may be able to withstand in the evil day,
and having done all ,
to stand.
Stand therefore,
having your loins girt about with truth,
and having on the breastplate of righteousness;
And your feet shod
with the " preparation of the gospel of peace " ;
Above all ,
taking the shield of faith,
wherewith ye shall be able to quench
all the fiery darts of the wicked.
And take the helmet of salvation,
and the sword of the Spirit,
which " is the word of God ".

Question: So does God mean that the whole armour is the whole word of God ?

God says in: St. Luke 4 : 4

And Jesus answered him saying,
It is written,
that man shall not live by bread alone,
but
by every word of God.

Question: Won't we get tired of reading the "Word of God" all the time ?

God says in: Ecclesiastes 12: 12

And further,
by these,
my son be admonished:
of making many books there is no end ;
and much study is a weariness of the flesh.

Question: So then why does God want us to study every word of the Bible ?

God says in: 2 Timothy 2 : 15

Study to show thyself approved
unto God ,
a workman that needeth not to be ashamed ,
rightly dividing the word of truth.

Chapter 4

(First Principle)

Repentance from dead works

(from acts that lead to death)

The Doctrine of Christ
Ronald F. Peters

Question: Is it really necessary to repent ?

God says in: 2 Peter 3 : 3 – 9

Knowing this first,
that there shall come in the last days
scoffers,
walking after their own lusts,
and saying ,
where is the promise of his coming ?
for since the fathers fell asleep,
all things continue as they were
from the beginning of the creation.
For this,
they willingly are ignorant of ,
that by the word of God
the heavens were of old ,
and the earth
standing out of the water
and in the water:
whereby the world that then was,
being overflowed with water, (Noah's flood)
perished:
But
the heavens and the earth ,
which are now,
by the same word
are kept in store,

reserved unto fire
against the day of judgment and perdition
of ungodly men.

But, beloved,
be not ignorant of this one thing ,
that one day is with the Lord as a thousand years,

and a thousand years as one day.
The Lord is not slack concerning his promise,
as some men count slackness;
But
is longsuffering to us-ward ,
not willing
that any should perish,
but
that all should "come to repentance " .

Question: How should people come to repentance ?

God says in: St Mark 1: 14 – 15

Now after that
John was put in prison,
Jesus came into Galilee,
preaching the gospel
of the Kingdom of God,
and saying ,
the time is fulfilled,
and the kingdom of God is at hand:
repent ye
and believe the gospel.

Question: So is believing the gospel part of repentance ?

God says in: The Acts 26 : 19 – 20

Whereupon , O King Agrippa ,
I was not disobedient unto the heavenly vision:
but shewed first unto them of Damascus,
and at Jerusalem, and throughout all the coasts of Judaea,
and then to the Gentiles,
that they should
repent
turn to God
and do works meet for repentance.

Question: What kind of works does God want us to do to show that we are repenting ?

God says in: St. Luke 19 : 2 - 9

And behold,
there was a man named Zacchaeus,
which was the chief among the publicans,
and was rich.
And he sought to see Jesus who he was;
and could not
for the press,
because he was little of stature.

and he ran before,
and climbed up into a sycamore tree to see him:
for he was to pass that way .

And when Jesus came to the place,
he looked up and saw him ,
and said unto him ,
Zacchaeus, make haste,
and come down,
for today I must abide at thy house.
And he made haste,
and came down ,
and received him joyfully.
And when they saw it ,
they all murmured,saying ,
that he was gone to be a guest
with a man that is a sinner.
And Zacchaeus stood,
and said unto the Lord;
behold Lord,
the half of my goods
I give to the poor

and
if I have taken any thing from any man
by false accusation,
I restore him fourfold.
And Jesus said unto him ,
this day is salvation come to this house
For so much as he also is a son of Abraham.

Question: Does repenting mean that we make things right before we continue with God ?

God says in: St. Luke 3 : 8 – 14

Bring forth therefore fruits worthy of repentance,
and begin not to say within yourselves,
we have Abraham to our Father :
for I say unto you ,
that God is able of these stones
to raise up children unto Abraham.

And now also the axe is laid
unto the root of the trees:
every tree therefore which bringeth not forth good fruit
is hewn down,
and cast into the fire.

And the " people " asked him,
saying "what shall we do then" ?
He answereth and saith unto them,
he that hath two coats,
let him impart to him that hath none;
and he that hath meat,
let him do likewise.

Then came also the " publicans " to be baptized,
and said unto him,
"Master, what shall we do" ?
And he said unto them,
exact no more than that which is appointed you.

And the " soldiers " likewise demanded of him ,
saying, " and what shall we do" ?
And he said unto them ,
do violence to no man,
neither accuse any falsely
and be content with your wages.

Question: Is there anything else that God wants us to do when we repent ?

God says in: The Acts 2 : 38

Then Peter said unto them,
repent ,
and be baptized everyone of you
in the name of Jesus Christ

for the remission of sins,

and ye shall receive the gift
of the Holy Ghost .

Question: Do people that are Christians need to repent too.

God says in: Revelation 2 : 4 – 7

Nevertheless I have somewhat against thee,
because thou hast left thy first love.

Remember therefore, from whence thou art fallen,
and repent,
and do the first works;
or else I will come to thee quickly,
and will remove thy candlestick
out of his place,
except thou repent.

But this thou hast,
that thou hatest the deeds
of the Nicolaitans,
which I also hate. (not the Nicolaitans , the deeds)

He that hath an ear,
let him hear what the Spirit saith
unto the churches;
to him that overcometh
will I give to eat of the tree of life,
which is in the midst of the paradise of God.

Question: What exactly does God expect people to do, when repenting ?

God says in: 2 Corinthians 7 : 9 – 11

Now I rejoice,
not that ye were made sorry,
but that ye sorrowed to repentance:
for ye were made sorry
after a godly manner,
that ye might receive damage by us in nothing .

For godly sorrow
worketh repentance to salvation
not to be repented of:
but the sorrow of the world worketh death.

For behold this selfsame thing,
that ye sorrowed after a godly sort,
what carefulness it wrought in you ,

yea,
what a clearing of yourselves,

yea,
what indignation,

yea,
what fear,

yea,
what a vehement desire,

yea,
what zeal,

yea,

what revenge !
In all things ye have approved yourselves
to be clear in this matter.

Question: How do people get motivated,
to want to repent ?

God says in: Romans 2: 4

Or despises thou the riches
of his goodness
and forbearance
and longsuffering;
not knowing that the goodness of God
leadeth thee to repentance .

Question: Who does God lead to repentance ?

God says in: St Mark 2 : 17

When Jesus heard it,
He saith unto them,

They that are whole
have no need of the physician,
but they that are sick :
I came not to call the righteous,
but sinners to repentance.

Question: What happens in heaven
when a person repents ?

God says in: St Luke 15 : 7

I say unto you ,
that likewise joy shall be in heaven
over one sinner that repenteth,
more than over ninety and nine just persons,
which need no repentance.

Chapter 5
(Second principle)

Of faith toward God

The Doctrine of Christ
Ronald F. Peters

Question: What is faith ?

God says in: Hebrews 11 : 1

Now faith is the substance of things hoped for , the evidence of things not seen

Question: Does God care whether we have faith or not ?

God says in: Hebrews 11: 6

But without faith
it is impossible to please him:
for he that cometh to God
must believe :
1. that he is,
and
2. that he is a rewarder
of them that diligently seek him.

Question: How does a person get faith ?

God says in: Romans 10: 15 – 17

And how shall they preach ,
except they be sent?
As it is written ,
how beautiful are the feet of them that preach
the gospel of peace,
and
bring glad tidings of good things !

But
they have not all obeyed the gospel.
For Esaias saith ,
Lord, who hath believed our report ?

So then
" Faith cometh by hearing " ,
and
hearing by the word of God.

Question: Does acquiring faith have any rules ?

God says in: James 1 : 5 - 8

If any of you lack wisdom ,
let him ask of God,
that giveth to all men liberally,
and upbraideth not,
and it shall be given him.

But let him
" ask in faith , nothing wavering " .
For he that wavereth
is like a wave of the sea
driven with the wind and tossed.

For let not that man
think that he shall receive anything
of the Lord.

A double minded man
is unstable in all his ways.

Question: How do we know that God
will send us something good,
if we exercise faith in him ?

God says in: James 1 : 17

Every good gift
and every perfect gift
is from above,
and cometh down
from the Father of lights,
with whom is no variableness,
neither shadow of turning.

Question: Can people get things from God without faith ?

God says in: Deuteronomy 32 : 20

And he said ,
I will hide my face from them
I will see what their end shall be:
for they are a very froward generation,
children in whom is no faith .

Question: So how much are we to exercise our faith in God ?

God says in: Habakkuk 2 : 4

Behold,
his soul which is lifted up
is not upright in him:
But the just
shall live by his faith .

Question: How exactly does this faith in God work ?

God says in: St. Mark 11 : 22 – 24

And Jesus answering saith unto them ,
have faith in God.

For verily I say unto you,
that whosoever shall

1) say unto this mountain,
   be thou removed,
   and be thou cast into the sea;
   and

2) shall not doubt in his heart,
   but

3) shall believe that those things
which he saith shall come to pass;

4) he shall have whatsoever he saith.

> Therefore I say unto you (because of the formula above)
> what things soever ye desire,
> when ye pray,
> believe that ye receive them,
> and ye shall have them .

Question: What other kinds of things can we do with faith ?

God says in: St Luke 17 : 5 - 6

And the apostles said unto the Lord,
increase our faith .

And the Lord said,
if ye had faith
as a grain of mustard seed,
ye might say unto this sycamine tree,
be thou plucked up by the root,
and be thou planted in the sea,
and it should obey you.

Question: Did King Jesus actually promise us
that we could do these kind of special things ,
if we did them by faith ?

God says in: St John 14 : 12 - 15

Verily , verily I say unto you,
He that believeth on me ,
the works that I do,
shall he do also ;
and greater works than these shall he do ;
because I go unto my Father.

And whatsoever ye shall ask
in my name
that will I do ,
that the Father may be glorified in the Son.

If ye ask anything in my name,
I will do it.

If ye love me ,
keep my commandments.

Question: Does that mean that , all we have to do is :
believe on King Jesus
and have faith
and every time
we just get what we ask ?

God says in: St John 15 : 1 - 7

I am the vine,
and my Father is the Husbandman.
Every branch in me
that beareth not fruit
He taketh away:

And every branch that beareth fruit,
He purgeth it
that it may bring forth more fruit.
Now ye are clean
through the word
which I have spoken unto you.

Abide in me , and I in you .

As a branch cannot bear fruit of itself,
except it abide in the vine;
no more can ye,
except ye abide in me.
I am the vine,
ye are the branches:

He that abideth in me,
and I in him,
the same bringeth forth
much fruit :
for without me
ye can do nothing.
If a man abide not in me

he is cast forth as a branch ,
and is withered;
and men gather them,
and cast them into the fire,
If
ye abide in me,
and my words abide in you,
ye shall ask what ye will,
and it shall be done unto you.

Question: Is there anything else that
King Jesus expects us to do,
so that we can actually
ask things and get real results ?

God says in: St. John 15 : 16

Ye have not chosen me,
but I have chosen you,
and ordained you,

That ye should go - (leave your house)
and
bring forth fruit - (bring in new Christians)
and
that your fruit should remain - (nuture and teach)

that
whatsoever ye shall ask
of the Father
in my name,
he may give it you .

Question: So then,
do we need to do all these things
for faith to work ?

God says in: James 2 : 17 - 22

Even so faith ,
if it hath not works,
is dead,
being alone.

Yea,
a man may say,
thou hast faith
and I have works:
show me thy faith without thy works ,
and

I will show thee my faith by my works.

Thou believest that there is one God;
thou doest well :

the devils also believe,
and tremble.

But wilt thou know ,
O vain man,
that faith without works is dead ?

Was not Abraham our father justified by works,
when he had offered Isaac, his son
upon the alter ?

Seest thou how faith
wrought with his works ,
and by works was faith made perfect ?

Question: Does God always benefit us when we have faith with works ?

God says in: Hebrews 6 : 10 - 12

For God is not unrighteous
to forget your work
and labour of love,

which ye have showed
toward his name,

in that
ye have ministered
to the saints,
and do minister.

And we
desire that every one of you

do show the same diligence
to the full assurance
of hope to the end:

That ye
be not slothful,
but followers
of them
who through
" faith and patience "
inherit the promises.

Chapter 6
(third principle)

The Doctrine of Water Baptism

The Doctrine of Christ
Ronald F. Peters

Authors note: In Hebrews chapter 6:2 it says :
"of the doctrine of Baptisms".
It specifically refers to more than one Baptism.

Therefore, in this book we will deal with both
1. the doctrine of "Water Baptism"
2. the doctrine of the "Baptism of the Holy Spirit".

They are very different,
and there are very specific reasons for both.

They are not given at the same time,
and they are not given the same way.

Many sincere Christians have denied
the Baptism of the Holy Spirit with various reasons.
Some have thought it will cause them embarrassment.
Others are afraid that they will need to use the gifts
of the Holy Spirit, like tongues and prophecy,
and they might do it badly.
Still others have been taught by their church
that it is cultish, and actually sinful to operate in the
gifts of the Holy Spirit.
Some believe that this was only for the Apostles
and first Christians,
and has nothing to do with Christians in this day and age.

What is amazing,
is that Christians all over the world
have not understood
that when you are given the "Baptism of the Holy Spirit",
and this follows with the gifts of the Holy Spirit,
that these gifts are not operated on
human power,

or human wisdom,
or on human skills,
or on human education,
but
by the unction
and leading
and literally by the "Holy Spirit" now in you.

Therefore ,
Chapter 5 expounds the reason for "Water Baptism"
Chapter 6 expounds the reason for " the Baptism of the Holy Spirit"

Question: After we get saved
by believing what King Jesus did for us,
is it then necessary to get
"water baptized"
and get the "Baptism of the Holy Spirit"

God says in: St. John 3 : 5 - 7

Jesus answered,
Verily, verily, I say unto thee,
except a man be

1. " born of water "

and

2. " of the Spirit ",

3. " he cannot enter into the kingdom of God ".
That which is born of the flesh is flesh;
and that which is born of the Spirit is spirit.

Marvel not that I said unto thee,
ye must be born again. (the Greek says " born from above")

Question: In order to be born again,
shouldn't we have to die first,
to be born again?

God says in: 2 Timothy 2 : 11

It is a faithful saying:
For if we be dead with him,
we shall also live with him.

Question: So how do we get to be dead with King Jesus ?

God says in: Romans 6 : 3 - 11

Know ye not,
that so many of us that were "baptized into Jesus Christ"
were baptized into his death ?

Therefore
" we are buried with him by baptism into death " :
that
like as Christ was raised up from the dead
by the glory of the Father,
even so we also
should walk in newness of life.

For if we have been
" planted together in the likeness of his death " ,
we shall be also
in the likeness of his resurrection:
Knowing this,
that our old man is crucified with him,
" that the body of sin might be destroyed " ,
that henceforth
we should not serve sin.

" For he that is dead is freed from sin ".

Now " if we be dead with Christ ,
we believe that we shall also live with him " :
knowing that Christ being raised from the dead ,
dieth no more;
death hath no more dominion over him.
For in that he died,
he died unto sin once:
but in that he liveth ,

he liveth unto God.
Likewise reckon ye also yourselves to be
dead indeed unto sin,
but alive unto God
through Jesus Christ our Lord.

Question: Is " to be born of water "
part of our Salvation process ?

God says in: 1 Peter 3 : 17 - 22

For it is better ,
if the will of God be so,
that ye suffer for well doing,
than evil doing.

For Christ also hath once suffered for sins,
the just for the unjust,
that he might
" bring us to God ,
being put to death in the flesh " ,
but quickened by the Spirit:

By which also he went
and preached unto the Spirits in prison; (in Hell)
which sometime were disobedient,
when once the longsuffering of God waited
in the days of Noah,
while the ark was a preparing,
wherein few,
that is ,
eight souls were saved by water.

The like figure
" whereunto even baptism doth also now save us "
(Not the putting away of the filth of the flesh ,
but
the answer of a good conscience toward God ,)
by the resurrection of Jesus Christ:
who is gone
into heaven,
and is on the right hand of God;

angels
and authorities
and powers
being made subject unto him.

Question: Should water baptism be
walking right out into the water
and then get put under it ?

God says in: St. Matthew 3 : 13 - 17

Then cometh Jesus from Galilee to Jordan unto John,
to be baptized of him.
But
John forbade him,
saying,
I have need to be baptized of thee,
and comest thou to me?

And Jesus answering said unto him,
suffer it to be so now:
for thus it
becometh us
to "fulfil all righteousness ".
(all of your unrighteousness gets permanently removed.)

Then he suffered him. (John said, " OK Jesus , lets go do it.")

And Jesus,
when he was baptized,
went up straightway " out of the water " :
and , lo,
the heavens were opened unto him,
and he saw the "Spirit of God "
descending like a dove,
and lighting upon him:
and lo, a voice from heaven
saying,

This is my beloved Son,
in whom I am well pleased.

Footnote: This is exactly what "The Father" says to everyone that gets baptized .

Question: When King Jesus came up out of the water ,
the spirit of God descended on him ,
which would be the Holy Spirit
and then God himself said :
" this is my beloved son ,
in whom I am well pleased ."

Does the same thing happen to us ,
when we get water baptized ?

Does God actually say out loud ,
this is my beloved son or daughter,
in whom I am well pleased ?

God says in: Galatians 4 : 4 – 7

But when the fullness of the time was come,
God sent forth his Son,
made of a woman ,
made under the law,
to redeem them that were under the law,
that we might receive the adoption of sons.

And because ye are sons,
God hath sent forth
the "Spirit of his son"
into your hearts ,
crying, Abba Father ,
Wherefore thou art no more a servant,
but a son ;
and if a son ,
then an heir of God
through Christ

Question: Is the "Spirit of God"
and the "Spirit of Christ" the same person ?

God says in: The Acts 2 : 38

Then Peter said unto them,
repent ,
and be baptized every one of you
in the name of Jesus Christ
for the remission of sins,
and ye shall receive the gift of the Holy Ghost.

Question: If God sends the Spirit of his Son into our hearts
when we come up out of the water ,
then does God join us to this Spirit
so that he can adopt us
into his Royal family ?

God says in: Romans 8 : 9 - 17

But ye are not in the flesh,
but in the Spirit,
if so be that the "Spirit of God dwell in you". (The Holy Spirit)

Now if any man have not the "Spirit of Christ",
he is none of his.

And if "Christ be in you", (the spirit of Christ)
the body is dead because of sin;
but the Spirit is life because of righteousness.

But
if the "Spirit of him"
that raised up Jesus from the dead "dwell in you",
 (the Spirit of God)
he that raised up Christ from the dead
shall also quicken your mortal bodies
by " his spirit that dwelleth in you."

Therefore ,
brethren ,
we are debtors ,
not to the flesh ,
to live after the flesh .
For if
ye live after the flesh .
ye shall die:
but if

ye through the Spirit
do mortify the deeds of the body ,
ye shall live .

For a many as are led by the Spirit of God,
they are the sons of God .

For ye have not received again
the spirit of bondage again to fear ;
but ye have received
the Spirit of adoption,
whereby we cry ,
Abba, Father .

The Spirit itself beareth witness with our spirit ,
that we are the children of God.

And if children ,
then heirs ;
heirs of God,
and joint-heirs with Christ ;
if so be that we suffer with him ,
that we may also be glorified together .

Question: Does King Jesus actually come to live inside us when we get water baptized?

God says in: Galatians 2 : 20

For I am crucified with Christ
nevertheless I live ;
yet not I ,
but Christ liveth in me :
and the life which I now live in the flesh
I live by the faith of the Son of God
who loved me,
and gave himself for me.

Question: Who is entitled to get water baptized ?

God says in: The Acts 8 : 35 - 39

Then Philip opened his mouth ,
and began at the same scripture,
and
preached unto him Jesus.

And
as they went on their way,
they came unto a certain water:
and the Eunuch said,
see, here is water;
what doth hinder me to be baptized?
(the question is really " who is entitled to be baptized")

And Philip said,
if thou believest with all thine heart , thou mayest.
And he answered and said,
I believe that Jesus Christ is the Son of God.
(He gave the right answer,
 because Philip baptized him.)

And he commanded the chariot to stand still
" and they went down both into the water ",
both Philip and the Eunuch;
and he baptized him.

And when they were come " up out of the water ",
the Spirit of the Lord caught away Philip,
that the Eunuch saw him no more:
And he went on his way rejoicing.

Authors note: How old do you need to be
to get water baptized ?
Old enough to
believe with all your heart
that Jesus Christ
is the Son of God.

Question: What is water baptism really for ?

God says in: Galatians 3 : 25 – 27 :

But after that faith is come,
we are no longer under a school master.
For ye are all children of God (how)
by faith in Christ Jesus.

For as many of you
" as have been baptized into Christ
have put on Christ " .

Question: Does this mean that in water baptism
we get married to King Jesus
and we become one flesh
just like in man and wife marriage ?

God says in: Ephesians 5 : 29 - 32

For no man ever hated his own flesh ;
But nourisheth and cherisheth it ,
even as the Lord the church :
For we are members of his body ,
Of his flesh,
And of his bones.
For this cause
shall a man leave his father and mother ,
and shall be joined unto his wife,
and they two
shall be one flesh.
This is a great mystery :
But I speak concerning Christ and the Church

Question: How was the first Covenant accepted, validated, and made legally binding with God?

God says in: Genesis 17 : 7 to 14

> And I will establish my covenant
> between me and thee
> and thy seed after thee in their generations
> for an everlasting covenant,
> to be a God unto thee,
> and to thy seed after thee.
>
> And I will give unto thee,
> And to thy seed after thee,
> the land wherein thou art a stranger
> all the land of Canaan,
> for an everlasting possession ;
> and I will be their God .
> And God said unto Abraham ,
> Thou shalt keep my covenant therefore ,
> thou,
> and thy seed after thee in their generations.
>
> This is my covenant,
> which ye shall keep,
> between me and you and thy seed after thee;
> Every man child among you shall be circumcised.
>
> And ye shall circumcise the flesh of your foreskin;
> And it shall be a token of the covenant
> betwixt me and you.
> And he that is eight days old .
> shall be circumcised among you,
> every man child in your generations ,
> he that is born in the house ,
> or bought with money of any stranger,
> which is not of thy seed .

He that is born in thy house,
and he that is bought with thy money,
must needs be circumcised:
and my covenant shall be in your flesh
for an everlasting covenant.

And the uncircumcised man child
whose flesh of his foreskin is not circumcised,
that soul shall be cut off from his people;
he hath broken my covenant.

Question: How is the new Covenant accepted, validated, and made legally binding with God ?

God says in: Colossians 2 : 8 - 15

> Beware
> lest any man spoil you
> through philosophy and vain deceit,
> after the tradition of men,
> after the rudiments of the world,
> and not after Christ.
> For in him dwelleth
> all the fulness of the Godhead bodily.
>
> And ye are complete in him,
> which is the head of all principality and power:
>
> In whom ye are circumcised
> with the circumcision made without hands
> in putting off the body of the sins of the flesh
>
> " by the circumcision of Christ:
> buried with him in baptism " ,
>
> wherein also ye are risen with him
> through the faith of the " operation of God "
> who hath raised him from the dead.

And you,
being dead in your sins
and the uncircumcision of your flesh,

hath he " quickened together with him ",

having forgiven you all trespasses;
" Blotting out
the handwriting of ordinances
that was against us ",
which was contrary to us,
and took it out of the way,
nailing it to his cross;

And having spoiled principalities and powers,
he made a shew of them openly,
triumphing over them in it.

Question: Does water baptism really blot out our sins ?

God says in: The Acts 22 : 11 - 16

And when I could not see for the glory of that light,
being led by the hand of them that were with me,
I came into Damascus.
And one Ananias,
a devout man according to the law,
having a good report of all the Jews which dwelt there,
Came unto me, and stood,
and said unto me,
Brother Saul, receive thy sight.
And the same hour I looked up upon him.
And he said, The God of our fathers hath chosen thee,
that thou shouldest know his will,
and see that Just One,
and shouldest hear the voice of his mouth.
For thou shalt be his witness
unto all men of what thou hast seen and heard.
And now , why tarriest thou?
" arise, and be baptized ,
and wash away thy sins " ,
calling on the name of the Lord.

Authors note: Remember that Christ Jesus said ,
"thus it becometh us to fulfil all righteousness",
St. Matthew 3 : 15
meaning - all unrighteousness gets removed.

Question: Once people understood
that they were to be baptized
by being buried under the water ,
into Jesus' death ,
and rise with him
by coming up out of the water ,
did they start baptizing
in " the name of the Lord Jesus " ?

God says in: The Acts 19 : 3 – 5

And he said unto them,
Unto what then were ye baptized?
And they said,
Unto John's baptism.
Then said Paul,
John verily baptized with the baptism of repentance,
saying unto the people,
that they should believe on him
which should come after him,
that is, on Christ Jesus.
When they heard this,
" they were baptized in the name of the Lord Jesus " .

Question: Who may get water baptized ?

God says in: The Acts 8 : 12

But " when they believed " Philip
preaching the things concerning the kingdom of God,
" they were baptized ",
both men and women.

Question: Is water baptism part of getting saved ?

God says in: St. Mark 16 :16

" He that believeth and is baptized shall be saved " ;
but
he that believeth not
shall be damned .

Question: How soon after people get saved should people be water baptized ?

God says in: The Acts 16 : 30 - 33

And brought them out,
and said, Sirs,
what must I do to be saved?

And they said,
Believe on the Lord Jesus Christ,
and thou shalt be saved,
and thy house.
And they spake unto him the word of the Lord,
and to all that were in his house.

And he took them " the same hour of the night ",

and washed their stripes;
and
" was baptized ,
he and all his ,
straightway " .

And when he had brought them into his house,
he set meat before them,
and rejoiced,
believing in God with all his house.

Question: So right after people get saved ,
should they should be taught
why they need to be water baptized,
and then, should we baptize them ?

God says in: The Acts 18 : 8

And Crispus,
the Chief Ruler of the Synagogue,
believed on the Lord with all his house;
and many of the Corinthians

1. hearing

2. believed,

3. and were baptized.

Authors note: People get saved,
and shortly thereafter
begin to falter ,
and the devil takes full advantage and tempts them,
in that area, where they are weak.

And soon, the Christian community scorns ,
and says that person wasn't very serious about his salvation.
But the newly saved person, has little power to fight the tempter,
because he has not "put on Christ".

We have just learned that we are to get baptized
by being buried with Christ ,
into his death ,
and then rising with Christ
into the newness of his life
being born again
by putting on the Spirit of Christ.

We learned, that
he that is dead, is freed from sin .
We learned that if we have been
"planted together" in the likeness of his death
we shall also be "in the likeness of his resurrection".
God has never died .
And the Holy Spirit has never died.

We are buried together with Christ, into his death.
Not into Gods death .
Not into the Holy Spirits death.
They never died.
We are put under the water
in the name of the "Lord Jesus Christ".

Some people ask about St. Mathew 28 : 19 where it says - baptizing them
in the "name" of the Father , and of the Son , and of the Holy Ghost.

It does not say - baptizing them in the Father, Son and Holy Ghost.

The name of the Father is Jesus ……. St. John 14 : 9 - 11
The name of the Holy Spirit is Jesus ….. St. John 14 : 16 - 18

Chapter 7

(the third principle)

The Doctrine of the Baptism of the Holy Spirit

The Doctrine of Christ
Ronald F. Peters

Question: Who qualifies for the baptism of the Holy Spirit

God says in: The Acts 8 : 16 - 20

Now when the apostles which were at Jerusalem
heard that Samaria had received the word of God,
they sent unto them Peter and John:
Who ,
when they were come down,
prayed for them,
that they might receive the Holy Ghost:

(for as yet he was fallen (the Holy Spirit)
upon none of them:
only they were baptized (water baptized)
in the name of the Lord Jesus.)

Then laid they their hands on them,
and they received the Holy Ghost.

And when Simon saw
that through the " laying on of the apostles' hands "
the Holy Ghost was given,
he offered them money,
Saying, give me also this power,
that on whomsoever I lay hands,
he may receive the Holy Ghost.

But Peter said unto him,
Thy money perish with thee,
because thou hast thought
that the gift of God
may be purchased with money.

Thou hast neither part nor lot in this matter:
for thy heart is not right
in the sight of God.

Repent therefore
of this thy wickedness
and pray God,
if perhaps the thought of thine heart
may be forgiven thee.
For I perceive that thou art
in the gall of bitterness,
and in the bond of iniquity.

Question: What did King Jesus tell us to do,
to receive the baptism of the Holy Spirit,
and how do we know for sure
that we will get
the "Baptism of the Holy Spirit" ?

God says in: St Luke : 11: 9 - 13

And I say unto you,
Ask,
and it shall be given you;
seek,
and ye shall find;
knock,
and it shall be opened unto you.
For every one that asketh receiveth;
and he that seeketh findeth,
and to him that knocketh it shall be opened.
If a son shall ask bread of any of you that is a father,
will he give him a stone ?
or if he ask a fish,
will he for a fish give him a serpent ?
Or if he shall ask an egg,
will he offer him a scorpion ?

If ye then, being evil,
know how to give "good gifts" unto your children:
how much more shall your heavenly Father
give the Holy Spirit
to them that ask him ?

Question: What actually happens
when a person receives the the Holy Ghost
by the laying on of hands
by an anointed person.
(a person who has the "Baptism of the Holy Spirit")

God says in: The Acts 1 : 8

But ye shall receive power ,
after that the Holy Ghost is come upon you:
and ye shall be witnesses unto me
both in Jerusalem,
and in all Judea,
and in Samaria,
and unto the uttermost part of the earth.

Question: What kind of power was King Jesus talking about ?

God says in: The Acts 2 : 1 - 18

And when the day of Pentecost was fully come,
they were all with one accord in one place.
And suddenly there came a sound from heaven
as of a rushing mighty wind;
and it filled all the house where they were sitting.
And there appeared unto them cloven tongues
like as of fire,
and it sat upon each of them.
And they were all filled with the Holy Ghost,
and began to speak with other tongues,
as the Spirit gave them utterance.

And there were dwelling at Jerusalem Jews
devout men, out of every nation under heaven.
Now when this was noised abroad,
the multitude came together,
and were confounded ,
because
that every man heard them speak
in his own language.
And they were all amazed and marveled,
saying one to another,
Behold ,
are not all these which speak Galilaeans ?
And how hear we every man in our own tongue,
wherein we were born ?
Parthians
and Medes,
and Elamites,
and the dwellers in Mesopotamia,
and in Judea,
and Cappadocia, in Pontus,

and Asia.
Phrygia,
and Pamphylia, in Egypt,
and in the parts of Libya about Cyrene,
and strangers of Rome,
Jews and proselytes,
Cretes,
and Arabians,
we do hear them speak in our tongues
the wonderful works of God.
And they were all amazed,
and were in doubt,
saying one to another,
What meaneth this ?
Others mocking said,
these men are full of new wine.

But Peter ,
standing up with the eleven,
lifted up his voice,
and said unto them,
ye men of Judaea,
and all ye that dwell at Jerusalem,
be this known unto you,
and hearken to my words:
For these are not drunken,
as ye suppose ,
seeing it is but the third hour of the day.

But this is that
which was spoken
by the prophet Joel;

And it shall come to pass in the last days,
saith God,
I will pour out my Spirit upon all flesh:

and your sons
and your daughters
shall prophesy,
and your young men shall see visions,
and your old men shall dream dreams:
And on my servants
and on my handmaidens
I will pour out in those days of my Spirit ;
and they shall prophesy.

Question: What results did St. Paul have
when he layed hands on people
to receive the Baptism of the Holy Ghost ?

God says in: The Acts 19 : 1 – 6

And it came to pass,
while Apollos was at Corinth,
Paul having passed through the upper coasts
came to Ephesus:
and finding certain disciples,
He said unto them,
Have ye received the Holy Ghost
since ye believed ?
And they said unto him,
We have not so much as heard
whether there be any Holy Ghost.
And he said unto them,
Unto what then were ye baptized ?
And they said, Unto John's baptism.
Then said Paul,
John verily baptized with the baptism of repentance,
saying unto the people,
that they should believe on him
which should come after him,
that is ,
on Christ Jesus.
When they heard this ,
They were baptized in the name of the Lord Jesus.

And when Paul had laid his hands upon them,
The Holy Ghost came on them;
And they spake with tongues,
and prophesied.

Question: What else can be released by the laying on of hands ?

God says in: 1 Timothy 4 : 11 – 16

These things command and teach.

Let no man despise thy youth;
But be thou an example of the believers,
in word,
in conversation,
in charity,
in spirit,
in faith
in purity.

Til I come, (the obligation of the gift of Teaching)
give attendance :
a) to reading,
b) to exhortation,
c) to doctrine.

Neglect not the gift that is in thee,
which was given thee by prophecy,
with the " laying on of the hands of the presbytery " .

Meditate upon these things;
give thyself wholly to them;
that thy profiting may appear to all.

Take heed unto thyself,
and unto the doctrine;
continue in them:
for in doing this
thou shalt both save thyself
and them that hear thee.

Question: Does the person who laid hands on the person who received the "Baptism of the Holy Spirit"; also decide which of the gifts of the Holy Spirit this person should receive ?

God says in: 1 Corinthians 12 : 12 - 27

> For as the body is one,
> and hath many members,
> and all the members of that one body,
> being many,
> are one body:
> so also is Christ.
> For by one Spirit are we all baptized
> into one body,
> whether we be Jews or Gentiles,
> whether we be bond or free;
> and have all made to drink into one Spirit.
> For the body is not one member,
> but many.
> If the foot shall say ,
> because I am not the hand,
> I am not of the body;
> is it therefore not of the body ?
> And if the ear shall say,
> because I am not the eye,
> I am not of the body;
> is it therefore not of the body ?
> If the whole body were an eye,
> where were the hearing ?
> If the whole were hearing ,
> where were the smelling ?
>
> But now
> hath God set the members
> every one of them in the body,

as it hath pleased him.

And if they were all one member,
where were the body ?
But now are they many members ,
yet but one body.
And the eye cannot say unto the hand,
I have no need of thee :
nor again the head to the feet ,
I have no need of you.
Nay , much more those members of the body,
which seem to be more feeble,
are necessary:
And those members of the body,
which we think to be less honourable,
upon those we bestow more abundant honour;
and our uncomely parts
have more abundant comeliness.
For our comely parts have no need:
but God hath tempered the body together,
having given more abundant honour
to that part which lacked:
That there should be no schism in the body;
but that the members should have the same care
one for another .

Question: If our God asigns the various gifts
within each church body
has he given instruction
how we are to relate to each other ?

God says in: 1 Corinthians 12 : 26 -27

And whether one member suffer,
all the members suffer with it ;
or one member be honoured,
all the members rejoice with it.
Now are ye the body of Christ ,
and members in particular.

Question: 1 Corinthians chapter 12 starts out
by saying ,
Now concerning spiritual gifts,
brethren,
I would not have you ignorant.

It would seem to be important ,
when a church is put together
that the congregation (the body) watch for
the gifts that God sends to it.

At the end of the chapter ,
included in the eight spiritual gifts
are what God has actually set
in the church .
What precisely is included
in these eight "Spiritual Gifts" ?

God says in: 1 Corinthians 12 : 28 – 30

And God hath set some
in the church,
1. first Apostles
2. secondarily prophets
3. thirdly teachers
4. after that miracles,
5. then gifts of healings
6. helps
7. governments
8. diversities of tongues

Are all apostles ?
Are all prophets ?
Are all teachers ?
Are all workers of miracles ?
Have all the gifts of healing ?

Do all speak with tongues ?
Do all interpret ?

But covet earnestly the best gifts:
and yet show I unto you
a more excellent way.

Question: When people receive
the baptism of the Holy Spirit,
it is apparently possible
that one of the above gifts may be given to you.
Seminaries that teach how to set up a Church
should be looking at
the exact sequence that God has laid out.
When God hands out these gifts
and sets them in a church,
how do those people learn those gifts ?

God says in: St. John 14 : 26

But the comforter ,
which is the Holy Ghost,
whom the Father will send in my name,
he shall teach you all things,
and bring all things to your remembrance,
whatsoever I have said unto you.

Question: It is obvious that when a church body receives
the baptism of the Holy Spirit,
that they will have the ability
to operate in the gifts
of the Holy Spirit,
as God disperses them.
They will have Holy Spirit power
to heal the sick,
to speak words of wisdom,
to speak prophesy,
to do miracles,
to have special faith,
to have discernment of spirits,
to speak in tongues,
and to interpret tongues.

What are we to do
if some Christians refuse this power,
by refusing "the Baptism of the Holy Ghost" ?

God says in: 2 Timothy 3 : 1 – 5

This know also,
that in the last days
perilous times shall come.
For men shall be lovers of their own selves,
covetous,
boasters,
proud,
blasphemers,
disobedient to parents ,
unthankful,
unholy,
without natural affection,
trucebreakers,
false accusers,

incontinent,
fierce,
despisers of those that are good,
traitors,
heady,
highminded,
lovers of pleasures more than lovers of God;
Having a form of godliness,
but denying the power thereof :
from such turn away.

Question: Who is actually entitled
to receive the baptism of the Holy Spirit ?

God says in: The Acts 5 : 32

And we are his witnesses
of these things;
and so is also the Holy Ghost ,
whom God hath given
to them that obey him.

Question: When a person has received the baptism
of the Spirit of God ,
does his knowledge and teaching change ?

God says in: 1 Corinthians 2 : 4 – 14

And my speech and my preaching
was not with enticing words of man's wisdom,
but in demonstration of the Spirit and of power :
That your faith should not stand in the wisdom of men,
but in the power of God.
Howbeit
we speak wisdom
among them that are perfect:
yet not the wisdom
of this world ,
nor of the princes of this world,
that come to nought :
But we speak the wisdom of God
in a mystery,
even the hidden wisdom ,
which God ordained
before the world unto our glory:
which none of the princes of this world knew:
for had they known it,
they would not have crucified
the Lord of Glory .
But as it is written ,
Eye hath not seen,
nor ear heard,
neither have entered into the heart of man,
the things which God hath prepared
for them that love him .
But God hath revealed them
unto us by his Spirit :

for the Spirit searcheth all things,
yea,
the deep things of God.

For what man knoweth the things of a man,
save the Spirit of man which is in him ?
even so the things of God knoweth no man,
but the Spirit of God.

Now we have received ,
not the Spirit of the world,
but the Spirit which is of God;
that we might know the things
that are freely given to us of God.

Which things also we speak,
not in the words which man's wisdom teacheth,
but which the Holy Ghost teacheth
comparing spiritual things with spiritual.

But the natural man receiveth not
the things of the Spirit of God:
for they are foolishness unto him:
neither can he know them,
because they are spiritually discerned.

Question: Does God really care
if we have the baptism of the Holy Spirit
that we may receive the Holy Ghost ,
and that there be operations of the Holy Ghost ,
including prophesies ?

God says in: 1 Thessalonians 5 : 16 – 20

1. Rejoice evermore
2. Pray without ceasing
3. In everything give thanks:
 for this is the will of God
 in Christ Jesus concerning you
4. Quench not the Spirit
5. Despise not prophesyings.

Chapter 8

(fourth principle)

The "laying on of hands"

The Doctrine of Christ
Ronald F. Peters

Question: Did laying on of hands
start as a new thing
in the New Testament ?

God says in: Leviticus 4 : 3 - 4

If the priest that is anointed do sin
according to the sin of the people;
then let him bring for his sin,
which he hath sinned,
a young bullock without blemish
unto the Lord for a sin offering.
And he shall bring the bullock
unto the door of the tabernacle of the congregation,
before the Lord;
and shall lay his hand upon the bullock's head,
and kill the bullock before the Lord.

Question: Should only the priest be allowed to lay hands
on the offering's head ?

God says in: Leviticus 4: 15

And the elders of the congregation
shall lay their hands upon the head
of the bullock before the Lord:
and the bullock shall be killed before the Lord.

Question: Did only the priests and elders lay hands on offerings ?

God says in: Leviticus 4 : 22 - 24

When a ruler hath sinned,
and done somewhat through ignorance
against any of the commandments of the Lord his God
concerning things which should not be done,
and is guilty; or if his sin,
wherein he hath sinned come to his knowledge;
he shall bring his offering,
a kid of the goats, a male without blemish:
and he shall lay his hand upon the head of the goat,
and kill it in the place
where they kill burnt offering
before the Lord:
it is a sin offering.

Question: Could anyone else put their hands on a sin offering ?

God says in: Leviticus 4 : 27 - 29

And if any one of the common people sin
through ignorance,
while he doeth somewhat
against any of the commandments of the Lord
concerning things which ought not to be done,
and be guilty;
or if his sin ,
come to his knowledge:
then he shall bring his offering,
a kid of the goats, a female without blemish,
for his sin which he hath sinned.
And he shall lay his hand
upon the head of the sin offering,
and slay the sin offering
in the place of the burnt offering.

Question: Did they only bring bulls and goats for a sin offering ?

God says in: Leviticus 4 : 32 - 33

And if he bring a lamb for a sin offering,
he shall bring it a female without blemish.
and he shall lay his hand
upon the head of the sin offering,
and slay it for a sin offering
in the place where they kill the burnt offering.

Question: What was the purpose of laying hands on the head of the offering animal ?

God says in: Leviticus 16 : 21

And Aaron shall lay both his hands upon the head of the live goat,
and confess over him all the iniquities of the children of Israel,
and all their transgressions in all their sins,
putting them upon the head of the goat,
and shall send him away by the hand of a fit man into the wilderness:
and the goat shall bear upon him all their iniquities unto a land not inhabited:
and he shall let go the goat in the wilderness.

Question: Was their sin transferred onto the animal when they layed their hands on its head ?

God says in: Numbers 8 : 12

And the Levites shall lay their hands
upon the heads of the bullocks:
and thou shalt offer the one for a sin offering,
and the other for a burnt offering unto the Lord
to make an atonement for the Levites.

Question: So can sins be transferred only to animals by laying on of hands ?

God says in: Leviticus 24 : 11 – 16

And the Israelitish woman's son
"blasphemed the name of the Lord",
and "cursed".
And they brought him unto Moses:
(and his mother's name was Shelomith,
the daughter of Dibri, of the tribe of Dan:)
And they put him in a ward,
that the mind of the Lord
might be showed them.

And the Lord spake unto Moses, saying,
Bring forth him that hath cursed without the camp;
and let all that heard him,
lay their hands upon his head,
and let all the congregation stone him.

And thou shalt speak unto the children of Israel, saying,
Whosoever curseth his God shall bear his sin.

And he that blasphemeth the name of the Lord,
he shall surely be put to death,
and all the congregation shall certainly stone him:
as well the stranger,
as he that is born in the land,
when he blasphemeth the name of the Lord,
shall be put to death.

Question: So can the laying on of hands
on another persons head
transfer sin ?

God says in: 1 Timothy 5 : 19 - 22

Against and elder
receive not an accusation,
but before two or three witnesses.

Them that sin
rebuke before all,
that others also may fear.

I charge thee before God,
and the Lord Jesus Christ,
and the elect angels,
that thou observe these things
without preferring one before another,
doing nothing by partiality.

Lay hands suddenly on no man,
neither be partaker of others men's sins:
keep thyself pure.

Question: So when King Jesus touched people with his hands, did this release a transfer of power to heal them ?

God says in: St. Matthew 9: 18 - 26

While he spake these things unto them,
behold, there came a certain ruler,
and worshipped him,
saying,
My daughter is even now dead:
but come and lay thy hand upon her,
and she shall live.

And Jesus arose,
and followed him,
and so did his disciples.

And behold,
a woman which was diseased
with an issue of blood twelve years,
came behind him,
and touched the hem of his garment:

For she said within herself,
if I may but touch his garment
I shall be whole.

But Jesus turned him about,
and when he saw her,
he said, Daughter,
be of good comfort;
thy faith hath made thee whole.

And the woman was made whole
from that hour.

And when Jesus came into the ruler's house,

and saw the minstrels
and the people making a noise,
He said unto them,
Give place:
for the maid is not dead,
but sleepeth .
And they laughed him to scorn.

But when the people were put forth ,
he went in,
and took her by the hand,
and the maid arose.
And the fame hereof went abroad
into all that land.

Question: So, did King Jesus have so much power
that even touching his clothes
released healing power ?

God says in: St. Matthew 9 : 27 - 31

And when Jesus departed thence,
two blind men followed him ,
crying,
and saying,

Thou son of David,
have mercy on us.
And when he was come into the house,
the blind men came to him:
and Jesus saith unto them,

Believe ye that I am able to do this?

They said unto him,
yea Lord.
Then he touched their eyes,
saying,
according to your faith be it unto you.

And their eyes were opened;
and Jesus straitly charged them ,
saying,
see that no man know it.

But they ,
when they were departed ,
spread abroad his fame
in all that country.

Question: When we have put on Christ in water baptism ,
could we release power
when we lay hands on someone ?

God says in: St. Mark 16 : 15 - 20

And he said unto them,

Go ye into all the world,
and preach the gospel to every creature.

He that believeth and is baptized shall be saved;
but
he that believeth not
shall be damned.

And these signs shall follow them that believe;

1. In my name shall they cast out devils;

2. they shall speak with new tongues;

3. they shall take up serpents;

4. and if they drink an deadly thing, it shall not hurt them;

5. they shall lay hands on the sick, and they shall recover

So then after the Lord had spoken unto them,
he was received up into heaven,
and sat on the right hand of God.

And they
went forth,
and preached everywhere,
the Lord working with them,
and confirming the word
with signs following.

Amen.

Chapter 9
(fifth principle)

The resurrection from the Dead

The Doctrine of Christ
Ronald F. Peters

Question: Did King Jesus explain anything about the "resurrection of the dead" to us ?
God says in: St . Luke 20 : 27 - 38

Then came certain Sadducees,
which deny that there is any resurrection;
and they asked him ,
saying, Master,
Moses wrote unto us,
if any man's brother die without children,
that his brother should take his wife ,
and raise up seed unto his brother.
There were therefore seven brethren :
and the first took a wife
and he died without children.
And the second took her to wife, and he died childless.
And the third took her;
and in like manner the seven also :
and they left no children, and died.
Last of all the woman died also .

Therefore
in the resurrection
whose wife of them is she ?
For seven had her to wife.

And Jesus answering said unto them,
the children of this world marry,
and are given in marriage:
but they which shall be accounted worthy
to obtain that world ,
and the resurrection from the dead,
neither marry , nor are given in marriage:
neither can they die any more:
for they are equal unto the angels;
and are the children of God,

being the children of the resurrection.
Now that the dead are raised,
even Moses showed at the bush,
when he calleth the Lord
the God of Abraham ,
and the God of Isaac,
and the God of Jacob.
For he is not a God of the dead,
but of the living: for all live unto him.

Question:	What did King Jesus mean by " they which shall be accounted worthy to obtain that world, and the resurrection from the dead " ?
God says in:	St. Luke 14 : 12 – 14
	Then said he also, to him that bade him, when thou makest a dinner or a supper, call not thy friends, nor thy brethren, neither thy kinsmen, nor thy rich neighbours; lest they also bid thee again, and a recompence be made thee. But when thou makest a feast , call the poor, the maimed , the lame, the blind: and thou shalt be blessed; for they cannot recompense thee: for thou shalt be recompensed at the resurrection of the just.
Question:	How do we get to be "just" , so that we can be in the resurrection of the just ?
God says in:	Romans 4 : 20 - 25
	He staggered not at the promise of God through unbelief; but was strong in faith , giving glory to God; and being fully persuaded that ,

what he had promised,
he was able also to perform .

And therefore
it was imputed to him for righteousness.
Now, it was not written for his sake alone ,
that it was imputed to him;
but for us also,
to whom it shall be imputed,

if we believe on him
that raised up Jesus our Lord
from the dead;
who was delivered for our offences,
and was raised again for our justification .

Question: When Christian believers die
where do they go
until the resurrection ?

God says in: St Luke 23 : 39 – 43

And one of the malefactors which were hanged
railed on him ,
saying , If thou be Christ ,
save thyself and us.
But the other answering rebuked him ,
saying, Dost not thou fear God,
seeing thou art in the same condemnation ?
And we indeed justly ;
for we receive the due reward of our deeds:
but this man hath done nothing amiss.
And he said unto Jesus , Lord,
remember me
when thou comest into thy kingdom .
And
Jesus said unto him ,
verily I say unto thee,
" today shalt thou be with me
in Paradise " .

Question: Where is paradise ?

God says in: 2 Corinthians 12 : 1 – 4

It is not expedient for me doubtless to glory .
I will come to visions and revelations of the Lord.

I knew a man in Christ, above fourteen years ago
(whether in the body, I cannot tell;
or whether out of the body, I cannot tell
God knoweth) ;
Such an one caught up to the third heaven .
And I knew such a man ,
(whether in the body,
or out of the body,
I cannot tell:
God knoweth)
How that he was caught up into paradise,
And heard unspeakable words,
Which it is not lawful for a man to utter .

Question: What else do we know about paradise ?

God says in: Revelation 2 : 7

He that hath an ear,
let him hear
what the Spirit saith
unto the churches;

To him that overcometh
will I give to eat of the tree of life ,
which is in the midst of
the paradise of God.

Question: Does everyone go to paradise ?

God says in: St Luke 16 : 19 – 31

There was a certain rich man ,
which was clothed in purple and fine linen,
and fared sumptuously every day:
And there was a certain beggar named Lazarus ,
which was laid at his gate, full of sores,
and desiring to be fed with the crumbs
which fell from the rich man's table :
moreover the dogs came and licked his sores.
And it came to pass,
that the beggar died,
and was carried by the angels into Abrahams bosom:

the rich man also died ,
and was buried ;
and in hell he lift up his eyes,
being in torments ,
and seeth Abraham afar off ,
and Lazarus in his bosom .

And he cried and said ,
Father Abraham ,
have mercy on me ,
and send Lazarus,
that he may dip the tip of his finger in water,
and cool my tongue ;
for I am tormented in this flame .
But
Abraham said ,
Son,
remember that thou in thy lifetime receivedst
thy good things ,
and likewise Lazurus evil things :

but now he is comforted ,
and thou art tormented.

And beside all this ,
between us and you there is a great gulf fixed :
so that they which would pass from hence to you cannot;
neither can they pass to us ,
that would come from thence.

Then he said ,
I pray thee therefore, father ,
that thou wouldest send him to my fathers house:
for I have five brethren;
that he may testifiy unto them,
lest they also come into this place of torment .

Abraham said unto him,
they have Moses and the prophets ;
let them hear them.

And he said, nay, father Abraham:
but if one went unto them from the dead,
they will repent.

And he said unto him,
If they hear not Moses and the prophets,
neither will they be persuaded,
though one rose from the dead.

Question: What exactly happens to Christian people when they die ?

God says in: 1 Corrinthians 15 : 39 - 58

All flesh is not the same flesh:
but there is one kind of flesh of men ,
another flesh of beasts,
another of fishes ,
and another of birds .

There are also celestial bodies ,
and bodies terrestrial :

But
the glory of the celestial is one ,
and the glory of the terrestrial is another.

There is one glory of the sun,
and another glory of the moon,
and another glory of the stars:
for one star differeth from another star in glory.

So also is the resurrection of the dead
It is sown in corruption;
it is raised in incorruption:
it is sown in dishonour;
it is raised in glory:
it is sown in weakness;
it is raised in power :
it is sown a natural body;
it is raised a spiritual body.

There is a natural body,
and there is a spiritual body.

And so it is written,
The first man Adam was made a living soul;

the last Adam was made a quickening spirit.

Howbeit
that was not first which is spiritual,
but
that which is natural;
and afterward that which is spiritual.
The first man is of the earth,
earthy:
The second man is the Lord from heaven.

As is the earthy,
such are they also,
that are earthy:
and as is the heavenly,
such are they also that are heavenly.
And as we have borne the image of the earthy,
we shall also bear the image of the heavenly.

Now this I say, brethren ,
that flesh and blood
cannot inherit the kingdom of God;
neither doth corruption inherit incorruption .

Behold ,
I show you a mystery ;
We shall not all sleep,
but we shall all be changed,
in a moment ,
in the twinkling of an eye,
at the last trump:
for the trumpet shall sound,
and the dead shall be raised incorruptible ,
and we shall be changed.

For this corruptible must put on incorruption,

And this mortal must put on immortality .

So when this corruptible
shall have put on incorruption,
and this mortal shall have put on immortality,

then shall be brought to pass
the saying that is written,
death is swallowed up in victory.

O death ,
where is thy sting ?

O grave ,
where is thy victory ?

The sting of death is sin;
and the strength of sin is in the law .

But
thanks be to God,
which giveth us the victory
through our Lord Jesus Christ .

Therefore ,
my beloved brethren,
be ye steadfast,
unmoveable ,
always abounding
in the work of the Lord,
forasmuch as ye know that
your labour
is not in vain in the Lord.

Question: What will happen to the people that are sleeping in Christ Jesus in that place called paradise, when the resurrection occurs ?

God says in: 1 Thessalonians 4 : 13 – 17

> But,
> I would not have you to be ignorant ,
> brethren ,
> concerning them which are asleep ,
>
> that ye sorrow not,
> even as others which have no hope,
> for if we believe
> that Jesus died and rose again,
> even so them also
> which sleep in Jesus
>
> will God bring with him .
> For this we say unto you
> by the word of the Lord ,
>
> That we which are alive
> and remain
> unto the coming of the Lord
> shall not prevent them
> which are asleep.
>
> For the Lord himself
> shall descend from heaven
> with a shout,
> with a voice of the archangel
> and with the trump of God ;
> and the dead in Christ
> shall rise first :

Then we which are alive
and remain
shall be caught up together
with them in the clouds,
to meet the Lord in the air ,
and so shall we ever be with the Lord .

Wherefore
comfort one another with these words.

Question: When people stand before God and get judged,
how will God sort out the people that go to
the lake of fire,
and those that don't ?

God says in: Revelation 20 : 9 - 15

And they went up on the breadth of the earth
and compassed the camp of the saints about,
and the beloved city:
and fire came down from God out of heaven,
and devoured them.
And the devil that deceived them
was cast into the lake of fire and brimstone,
where the beast and the false prophet are,
and shall be tormented
day and night for ever and ever .
And
I saw a great white throne ,
and him that sat on it ,
from whose face
the earth and the heaven fled away;
and there was found no place for them.
And I saw the dead,
small and great,
stand before God;

and the books were opened
and another book was opened,
which is the book of life :

and the dead were judged out of those things
which were written in the books,
according to their works.
And the sea gave up the dead
which were in it ;

and death and hell delivered up the dead
which were in them:
and they were judged every man
according to their works.

And death and hell were cast into the lake of fire.
This is the second death .

And whosoever was not found
written in the book of life
was cast into the lake of fire.

Chapter 10

(Sixth principle)

Eternal Judgment

The Doctrine of Christ
Ronald F. Peters

Question: Who is this God
that executes "eternal judgment" ?

God says in: Deuteronomy 10 : 17 - 21

For the Lord your God is
God of gods,
Lord of lords
a great God,
a mighty ,
and a terrible,
which regardeth not persons,
nor taketh reward :

He doth execute
the judgment
of the fatherless and widow,
and loveth the stranger,
in giving him food and raiment .

Love ye therefore the stranger:
for ye were strangers in the land of Egypt.
thou shalt fear the Lord thy God;
Him shalt thou serve,
and to him shalt thou cleave,
and swear by his name.

He is thy praise ,
and he is thy God,
that hath done for thee
these great and terrible things,
which thine eyes have seen.

Question: How does God Judge people ?

God says in: Job 8 : 3 – 4

> Doth God pervert judgment ?
> Or doth the Almighty pervert justice ?
> If thy children have sinned against him ,
> and he have cast them away
> for their transgression .

Question: What kind of judge is God ?

God says in: Job 37 : 23

> Touching the Almighty ,
> we cannot find him out:
> he is excellent in power,
> and in judgment
> and in plenty of justice:
> he will not afflict.
>
> Men do therefore fear him:
> He respecteth not any
> that are wise of heart.

Question: How do the ungodly get judged ?

God says in: Psalms 1 : 4 - 6

> The ungodly are not so ;
> but are like the chaff
> which the wind driveth away.
> therefore the ungodly
> shall not stand in the judgment ,
> nor sinners
> in the congregation of the righteous.
> for the Lord knoweth the way of the righteous:
> but the way of the ungodly shall perish.

Question: What is God going to judge us for ?

God says in: Ecclesiastes 12 : 14

For
God shall bring every work
into judgment ,
with every secret thing ,
whether it be good ,
or whether it be evil.

Question: Where is this place ,
where God will judge us ?

God says in: Ecclesiastes 3 : 16 - 17

And moreover
I saw under the sun
the place of judgment ,

that wickedness was there ;
and the place of righteousness,
that iniquity was there .

I said in my heart,
God shall judge the righteous and the wicked:
for there is a time there
for every purpose
and for every work.

Question: What kind of things will God judge ?

God says in: St Matthew 12 : 36 – 37

But I say unto you ,
that every idle word
that men shall speak,
they shall give account thereof
in the day of judgment .
For by words
thou shalt be justified
and by words
thou shalt be condemned .

Question: What other things shall God judge us for ?

God says in: St Matthew 5 : 22

But I say unto you ,
that whosoever is angry with his brother
without a cause
shall be in danger of the judgment :
and whosoever shall say to his brother ,
Raca, (Raca = vain fellow)
shall be in danger of the council;
but whosoever shall say thou fool,'
shall be in danger of hell fire.

Question: For what sins
will God sentence people
to eternal death ?

God says in: Romans 1: 18 - 32

For the wrath of God
is revealed from heaven
against all ungodliness
and unrighteousness of men ,
who hold the truth in unrighteousness;
because that which may be known of God
is manifest in them;
for God hath shewed it unto them.
For the invisible things of him
from the creation of the world
are clearly seen,
being understood by the things that are made,
even his eternal power and Godhead;
so that they are without excuse :

Because that, when they knew God,
they glorified him not as God,
neither were they thankful;
but became vain in their imaginations,
and their foolish heart was darkened.
Professing themselves to be wise,
they became fools,
and changed the glory of the uncorruptible God
into an image made like to corruptible man,
and to birds,
and to fourfooted beasts,
and creeping things.

Wherefore
God also gave them up to uncleaness

through the lusts of their own hearts,
to dishonour their own bodies
between themselves:

who changed the truth of God into a lie,
and worshipped and served the creature
more than the Creator ,
who is blessed for ever. Amen

For this cause
God gave them up
unto vile affections:

for even their women
did change the natural use
into that which is against nature:

And likewise also the men ,
leaving the natural use of the woman ,
burned in their lust one toward another ;
men with men
working that which is unseemly,
and receiving in themselves
that recompence of their error
which was meet. (their fitting retribution)

And even as they did not like
to retain God in their knowledge ,

God gave them over to a reprobate mind,
to do those things which are not convenient;
being filled with all unrighteousness,

fornication,
wickedness,
covetousness,
maliciousness;

full of envy,
murder,
debate,
deceit,
malignity,
whisperers,
backbiters,
haters of God,
despiteful,
proud,
boasters,
inventors of evil things,
disobedient to parents,
without understanding,
covenant breakers,
without natural affection,
implacable,
unmerciful:
who knowing the judgment of God,
that they which commit such things
are worthy of death,
not only do the same,
but have pleasure in them that do them.
(consent to or watch the one's practicing these sins)

Question: Romans 1 : 21 says that " because
when they knew God, they glorified him not as God, and were not thankful ."
And in verse 26 " for this cause God gave them up unto vile affections: for even their women did change the natural use into that which is against nature:
and likewise also the men,
leaving the natural use of the woman,
burned in their lust toward one another.
And in verse 28 it also says ,
God gave them over to a reprobate mind ,
to do those things"
Does God actually give people a delusion that they believe a lie,
to think that they are naturally
perverted,
and for them it is not sin ?

God says in: 2 Thessalonians 2:10-12
And with all deceivableness
of unrighteousness
in them that perish;
because they have not received
the love of the truth,
that they might be saved.
And for this cause,
God shall send them
strong delusion;
that they should believe a lie:
that they all might be damned
who believe not the truth
but had pleasure in unrighteousness.

Question: Can we really be sure,
that
at the judgment of God,
he will actually punish people eternally?

God says in: 2 Peter 2 : 4 - 10

For if God spared not the angels
that sinned,
but cast them down to hell,
and delivered them
into chains of darkness,
to be reserved unto judgment;

and spared not the old world,
but saved Noah
the eighth person,
a preacher of righteousness,
bringing in the flood upon the world of the ungodly;

and turning the cities of Sodom and Gomorrha
into ashes,
condemned them with an overthrow,
making them an ensample
unto those that after,
should live ungodly;
and delivered just Lot,
vexed with filthy conversation of the wicked:
(for that righteous man dwelling among them,
in seeing and hearing,
vexed his righteous soul from day to day
with their unlawful deeds;)

The Lord knoweth how to deliver the godly
out of temptations,
and to reserve the unjust

                         unto the day of judgment
to be punished :

but chiefly them that walk after the flesh
in the lust of uncleaness,
and despise government,
presumptuous are they ,
selfwilled ,
they are not afraid
to speak evil of dignities.

Question: Can people escape
the eternal judgment of God ?

God says in: Romans 2 : 1 – 3

Therefore thou art inexcusable
O man ,
whosoever thou art that judgest:
for wherein thou judgest another ,
thou condemnest thyself;
for thou that judgest
doest the same things.
But
we are sure that the judgment of God
is according to truth
against them which commit such things .
And
thinkest thou this ,
O man ,
that judgest them which do such things,
and doest the same ,
that thou shalt escape the judgment of God ?

Question: Since nothing seems to have changed much
for 2000 years, why should we
really be concerned about eternal judgment ?

God says in: 2 Peter 3 : 3 – 13

Knowing this first,
that there shall come
in the last days
scoffers,
walking after their own lusts,
and saying,
where is the promise of his coming ?

For since the fathers fell asleep,
all things continue as they were
from the beginning of the creation .
For this they willingly are ignorant of ,
that by the word of God
the heavens were of old,
and the earth
standing out of the water
and in the water:
whereby the world that then was,
being overflowed with water ,
perished:
but the heavens and the earth ,
which are now,
by the same word
are kept in store ,
reserved unto fire
against the day of judgment
and perdition of ungodly men.

But,
beloved,
be not ignorant of this one thing ,
that one day is with the Lord
as a thousand years,
and a thousand years as one day.

The Lord is not slack
concerning his promise
as some men count slackness;
but is longsuffering to us-ward
not willing that any should perish,
but that all
should come to repentance .

But the day of the Lord will come
as a thief in the night ;
in the which ,
the heavens shall pass away ,
with a great noise,
and the elements shall melt
with fervent heat,
and the earth also
and the works that are therein
shall be burned up.

Seeing then
that all these things
shall be dissolved ,
what manner of persons ought ye to be
in all holy conversation and godliness,
looking for and hasting
unto the coming day of God,
wherein the heavens being on fire
shall be dissolved
and the elements

shall melt with fervent heat?

Nevertheless we ,
according to his promise,
look for new heavens
and a new earth,
wherein dwelleth righteousness.

My Friend

My friend, I stand in "the judgment" now,
and feel that you're to blame somehow.

On earth, I walked with you day by day
and never did you show me "the way".

You knew the Lord, in truth and glory,
but never did you tell me the story.

My knowledge then was very dim;
you could have led me safe to Him.

Though we lived together on the earth,
you never told me of this second birth,
and now I stand this day condemned,
because you failed to mention Him!

We worked by day and talked by night,
and yet you showed me not "the light".

You let me live, and love, and die,
and you knew I'd never live "on high"

Yes, I called you my friend in life,
and trusted you through joy and strife.

And yet in coming to this horrible end
can I now call you "my friend"?

Chapter 11

"New Testament" sin

The Doctrine of Christ
Ronald F. Peters

Question: Since most people don't know anymore ,
what is sin and what is not sin ,
should we concern ourselves about sins ?

God says in: Ecclesiastes 8: 11

Because sentence
against an evil work
is not executed speedily,
therefore the heart
of the sons of men
is fully set in them
to do evil.

(Another translation called "The Living Bible" says :
" Because God does not punish sinners instantly ,
people feel it is safe to do wrong" .)

Authors note:

Can you imagine ,
that,
if every time you sinned,
even just a lustful thought ,
God would immediately send
a severe electric shock into your brain,
that would make you sizzle with such pain,
that you would fall down
and scream to God for mercy.

But God has chosen
not to execute his judgment
until the end of this world.

Then
every thought you had,
every word you spoke ,
every deed you did,
every one you hurt,
every one you didn't help,
every day you neglected to involve God,
every sin you committed ,
is all written down in the books
that will be brought before God ,
and you
will be judged.

Question: Should only those people who have sinned be concerned ?

God says in: Romans 3 : 23

For all have sinned,
and come short of the glory of God .

Question: If all have sinned
is everyone guilty before God ?

God says in: Romans 3 : 9 - 20

What then ?
Are we better than they ?
No, in no wise:
for we have before proved both Jews and Gentiles,
that they are all under sin;
As it is written, there is none righteous,
no , not one :

There is none that understandeth ,
there is none that seeketh after God .
they are all gone out of the way,
they are together become unprofitable;
there is none that doeth good,
no, not one.

Their throat is an open sepulcher;
with their tongues they have used deceit;
the poison of asps is under their lips:
whose mouth is full of cursing and bitterness :
their feet are swift to shed blood:
destruction and misery are in their ways:
and the way of peace have they not known :
there is no fear of God before their eyes.

Now we know that what things soever the law saith ,
it saith to them who are under the law:
that every mouth may be stopped,
and all the world may become guilty before God.

Therefore
By the deeds of the law
there shall no flesh be justified in his sight :
for by the law is the knowledge of sin .

Question: If people have never heard the law of God are they still guilty of sin ?

God says in: Romans 2 : 12

For as many as have sinned
without the law
shall also perish without the law :

and

as many as have sinned in the law
shall be judged by the law.

Question: What happens to people who have sinned and have been judged guilty before God ?

God says in: Revelation 20 : 12 – 15

And I saw the dead,
small and great,
stand before God ;
and the books were opened :
and another book was opened,
which is the book of life :

and the dead were judged
out of those things
which were written in the books ,
according to their works.

And the sea gave up the dead which were in it ;
and death and hell delivered up the dead
which were in them:

and they were judged every man
according to their works.

And death and hell were cast into the lake of fire.

This is the second death .
And whosoever was not found written in the book of life
was cast into the lake of fire.

Question: How do we get our name written into the book of life ?

God says in: Malachi 3 : 16 - 18

Then they " that feared the Lord "
spake often one to another :
and the Lord hearkened,
and heard it ,
and a " book of remembrance "
was written before him
for them " that feared the Lord " ,
and " that thought upon his name " .

And they shall be mine,
saith the Lord of Hosts,
in that day when I make up my jewels;
and I will spare them ,
as a man spareth his own son
that serveth him.

Then shall ye return,
and discern
between the righteous and the wicked,

(what is the difference between
the righteous and the wicked)

between him that serveth God
and him that serveth him not.

Question: Has God provided an escape from the "eternal punishment of sin " ?.

God says in: St John 3 : 16 - 21

> For God so loved the world ,
> that he gave
> his only begotten son,
> that whosoever believeth in him
> should not perish,
> but have eternal life .
>
> For God sent not his Son into the world
> to condemn the world;
> but that the world
> through him might be saved .
> He that believeth on him
> is not condemned:
> but he that believeth not
> is condemned already, (why ?)
>
> because
> he hath not believed
> in the name
> of the only begotten Son of God .
>
> And this is the condemnation ,
>
> that light is come into the world ,
> and men loved darkness rather than light ,
> because their deeds were evil.
>
> For everyone that doeth evil
> hateth the light
> neither cometh to the light ,
> lest his deeds be reproved.
>
> But he that doeth truth ,

(truth is something we must do)
cometh to the light ,
that his deeds may be made manifest,
that they are wrought in God .

Authors note: Many books have been written,
debating the theology of God's grace.
We are not under the law
but under grace,
if in fact we have accepted
the blood of Christ Jesus
as the atonement for our sins.
However, the issue of sin still remains.
The law wasn't made for God's benefit.
Our sins don't actually effect God.
They only interfere
with our relationship with God.
These laws were made,
so that man could have a better life.
Disobedience of these laws
requires confession of the sin,
and repentance.

When I teach repentance,
I often use this illustration.
Let's say that I have stolen the pastors car.
After many weeks,
my conscience bothering me,
I finally confess to the pastor
that it was me that stole his car.
Being the fine fellow that he is,
he forgives me.
I feel relieved,
and go home
and keep the car.
Repentance has not been committed.

Both confession and repentance cannot be performed
if the person has no knowledge of the sin committed.
Therefore, for reparation and expiation,

to appeal for God's grace,
it became necessary to record the sins
listed in the New Testament.
I have never met anyone
that has totally stopped sinning.
I asked my senior pastor on one occasion,
If,
as you grow older,
is it easier to live without sin.
He said it actually becomes harder.

I am convinced,
that the more active a person is,
in servant mode,
to our Lord King Jesus,
the stronger the temptations become.

Everyone is weak in certain areas.
We don't all have the same temptations.
Grace is synonymous with liberty.

King Jesus says in : Galatians 5 : 13 – 14
For, brethren, ye have been called unto liberty;
only use not liberty for an occasion to the flesh,
but by love
serve one another.
For all the law is fulfilled in one word,
even in this;
Thou shalt love thy neighbour as thyself .

Question: What are these "New Testament" sins which will send us into eternal punishment ?

God says in:

1 - St Matthew 4 : 7 - Not tempt the Lord thy God (foolish tests)

2 - St Matthew 4 : 10 - thou shalt worship the Lord thy God and him only shalt thou serve ,

3 - St Matthew 5 : 21 - thou shalt not kill

4 - St. Matthew 5 : 22 - angry with his brother without cause

5 - St. Matthew 5 : 22 - whosoever shall say "thou fool"

6 - St. Matthew 5 : 27 - thou shalt not commit adultery

7 - St. Matthew 5 : 28 - looketh on a woman to lust after her

8 - St. Matthew 5 : 34 - swear not at all (do not bind yourself with an oath)

9 - St. Matthew 7 : 1 - judge not, that ye be not judged.

10 - St Matthew 12 : 32 - not speak against the Holy Ghost (blasphemy Colos. 3:8)

11 - St Matthew 15 : 4 - honour thy father and mother (2 Tim . 3 : 2)

12 - St Matthew 19 : 18 - thou shalt not steal

13 - St Matthew 19 : 18 - thou shalt not bear false witness

14 - StMatthew 19 : 19 - love thy neighbour as thyself

15 - St Matthew 22 : 37 - Thou shalt love the Lord thy God
> with all thy heart
> with all thy soul
> with all thy mind
> with all thy strength (St Mark 12 : 30)

16 - St Mark 10 : 11 - shall put away his wife and marry another committeth adultery against her

17 - St. John 13 : 34 - that ye love one another as I have loved you

18 - the Acts 15 : 29 - that ye abstain from meats offered to idols ,
and from blood, and from things strangled, and from fornication

19 - the Acts 23 : 5 - Thou shalt not speak evil of the ruler of thy people

20 - Romans 1 : 21 - when they knew God , they glorified him not as God

21 - Romans 1 : 21 - neither were thankful

22 - Romans 1 : 21 - became vain in their imaginations (James 3 : 13-17)

23 - Romans 1 : 22 - professing themselves to be wise

24 - Romans 1 : 23 - changed the glory of God into an image

25 - Romans 1 : 24 - changed the truth of God into a lie

26 - Romans 1 : 26 - woman did change the natural use

27 - Romans 1 : 27 - men with men - working that which is unseemly (Lev. 20: 13)

28 - Romans 1 : 28 - did not like to retain God in their knowledge

29 - Romans 1 : 29 - wickedness

30 - Romans 1 : 29 - covetousness (Hebrews 13 : 5)

31 - Romans 1 : 29 - malicioiusness

32 - Romans 1 : 29 - full of envy

33 - Romans 1 : 29 - murder

34 - Romans 1 : 29 - debate

35 - Romans 1 : 29 - deceit

36 - Romans 1 : 29 - malignity

37 - Romans 1 : 29 - whisperers (1 Tim . 5 : 13)

38 - Romans 1 : 30 - backbiters

39 - Romans 1 : 30 - haters of God

40 - Romans 1 : 30 - despiteful

41 - Romans 1 : 30 - proud

42 - Romans 1 : 30 - boasters

43 - Romans 1 : 30 - inventors of evil things

44 - Romans 1 : 30 - disobedient to parents

45 - Romans 1 : 31 - without understanding

46 - Romans 1 : 31 - covenantbreakers (1 Tim . 3 : 3)

47 - Romans 1 : 31 - without natural affection

48 - Romans 1 : 31 - implacable

49 - Romans 1 : 31 - unmerciful

50 - Romans 1 : 32 - have pleasure in them that do them (the things that are sin - above)

51 - 1 Corinthians 5 : 10 - extortioners

52 - 1 Corinthians 5 : 11 - railer

53 - 1 Corinthians 5 : 11 - drunkard

54 - 1 Corinthians 6 : 9 - effeminate

55 - 1 Corinthains 6 : 9 - abusers of themselves with mankind

56 - 1 Corinthians 6 : 10 - thieves

57 - 1 Corinthians 10 : 10 - murmurers (Jude 1 : 16)

58 - Ephesians 4 : 19 - lasciviousness (inciting to lust)

59 - Ephesians 5 : 3 - uncleanness

60 - Ephesians 5 : 4 - filthiness (Colossians 3 : 8)

61 - Ephesians 5 : 4 - foolish talking

62 - Ephesians 5 : 4 - jesting

63 - Ephesians 5 : 5 - whoremonger

64 - Ephesians 5 : 5 - idolater

65 - Colossians 3 : 5 - inordinate affection (1 Tim . 3:3)

66 - Colossians 3 : 5 - evil concupiscence

67 - Colossians 3 : 9 - lie not one to another

68 - 1 Timothy 1 : 10 - menstealers

69 - 2 Timothy 3 : 2 - lover of their own selves

70 - 2 Timothy 3 : 3 - incontinent

71 - 2 Timothy 3 : 3 - fierce

72 - 2 Timothy 3 : 3 - despisers of those that are good

73 - 2 Timothy 3 : 4 - Traitors

74 - 2 Timothy 3 : 4 - heady

75 - 2 Timothy 3 : 4 - highminded

76 - 2 Timothy 3 : 4 - lovers of pleasures more than lovers of God

77 - 2 Timothy 3 : 4 - having a form of Godliness but denying the power thereof

78 - Hebrews 12 : 25 - see that ye refuse not him that speaketh from heaven

79 - James 2 : 9 - if ye have respect to persons ye commit sin (predudice)

80 - Revelation 14 : 11 - whosoever receiveth the mark 666 (Rev . 13 :16-18)

81 - Revelation 21 : 8 - fearful

82 - Revelation 21 : 8 - unbelieving

83 - Revelation 21 : 8 - abominable

84 - Revelation 21 : 8 - sorcerers

85 - Revelation 22 : 15 - whosoever loveth and maketh a lie

Question: If a Christian
has commited one of these sins
what can he do ?

God says in: 1 John 1 : 9

If we confess our sins ,
He is faithful and just to forgive us our sins,
and
to cleanse us from all unrighteousness .

Chapter 12

Idols and Images

The Doctrine of Christ
Ronald F. Peters

Question: In what order of importance did God write the "ten commandments"?

God says in: Exodus 20: 3 – 17

1. Thou shalt have no other gods before me
2. Thou shalt not make unto thee any graven image
3. Thou shalt not take the name of the Lord thy God in vain
4. Remember the Sabbath day, to keep it Holy
5. Honour thy Father and thy Mother
6. Thou shalt not kill
7. Thou shalt not commit adultery
8. Thou shalt not steal
9. Thou shalt not bear false witness against thy neighbour
10. thou shalt not covet
    - thy neighbours house
    - thy neighbours wife
    - thy neighbours servants,
    - thy neighbours animals,
    or anything else.

Question: In the 10 commandments ,
also known as the "Decalogue,"
why did God
make his very first commandment
" not to have any other gods" ?

God says in: Exodus 20: 1 – 6

And God spake all these words,
saying ,
I am the Lord thy God,
which have brought thee out of the land of Egypt
out of the house of bondage

Thou shalt have no other gods before me.
Thou shalt not make unto thee any graven image ,
or any likeness of any thing
that is in heaven above,
or that is in the earth beneath,
or that is in the water under the earth :

Thou shalt not bow down thyself to them,
nor serve them:

(Why ?)

for I,
the Lord thy God
am a jealous God,

visiting the iniquity of the fathers
upon the children
unto the third and fourth generation (Wow)
of them that hate me;

and showing mercy unto thousands
of them that love me,
and keep my commandments.

Question: What does our Great God think of the other gods?

God says in: Exodus 23 : 13

And in all things
that I have said unto you
be circumspect:
and make "no mention of the name of other gods",
neither let it be heard out of thy mouth.

Question: What does God say about other gods?

God says in: Psalms 96 : 4 – 5

For the Lord is great,
and greatly to be praised :
He is to be feared above all gods.

(Why ?)

For all the gods of the nations are idols :
but the Lord made the heavens.

Question: What does God mean
by that statement :
"He made the heavens" ?

God says in: Isaiah 40 : 18 - 22

To whom then will ye liken God ?
or what likeness will ye compare unto him ?

The workman melteth a graven image ,
and the goldsmith spreadeth it over with gold,
and casteth silver chains .

He that is so impoverished
that he hath no oblation
chooseth a tree that will not rot;
he seeketh unto him a cunning workman
to prepare a graven image ,
that shall not be moved .

Have ye not known ?
have ye not heard ?
hath it not been told you from the beginning ?
have ye not understood from the foundations of the earth ?

It is he that sitteth upon the circle of the earth ,
and the inhabitants thereof are as grasshoppers ;
that stretcheth out the heavens as a curtain ,
and spreadeth them out as a tent to dwell in .

Question: What does God want us to do about the idols that exist ?

God says in: Exodus 23 : 24 – 25

Thou shalt not bow down to their gods ,
nor serve them ,
nor do after their works:
but thou shalt utterly overthrow them,
and quite break down their images.

And ye shall serve the Lord your God ,
and he shall bless thy bread,
and thy water ;
and I will take sickness away
from the midst of thee

Question: Does God want us to go into their land to do this , or is this only if they bring their idols into our land ?

God says in: Deuteronomy 7 : 3 - 6

Neither shalt thou make marriages with them ;
thy daughter thou shalt not give unto his son ,
nor his daughter shalt thou take unto thy son .

For they will turn away thy son
from following me ,
that they may serve other gods:
so will the anger of the Lord
be kindled against you ,
and destroy thee suddenly .

But thus shall ye deal with them ;
ye shall destroy their alters,
and break down their images ,
and cut down their groves,
and burn their graven images with fire.

Authors note: My presumption is to only break them down if they are brought onto your land.

Question: Were there any reprocussions when Christians spoke out against idols ?

God says in: the Acts 19 : 24 - 29

> For a certain man named Demetrius ,
> a silversmith
> which made silver shrines for Diana,
> brought no small gain unto the craftsmen ;
> whom he called together
> with the workmen of like occupation ,
> and said ,
> Sirs ,
> ye know that by this craft
> we have our wealth.
>
> Moreover ye see and hear ,
> that not alone at Ephesus ,
> but almost throughout all Asia,
> this Paul hath persuaded
> and turned away much people ,
> saying that they be no gods,
> which are made with hands:
> So that not only this
> our craft is in danger
> to be set at nought ;
> but also that the temple
> of the great goddess Diana
> should be despised,
> and her magnificence
> should be destroyed,
> whom all Asia
> and the world
> worshippeth .

> And when they heard these sayings,
> They were full of wrath,
> and cried out ,
> saying,
> Great is Diana of the Ephesians .
> And the whole city was filled with confusion:
> and having caught Gaius and Aristarchus ,
> men of Macedonia,
> Pauls companions in travel,
> they rushed with one accord
> into the theatre .

Question: What about if people that come into our land become Christians ?

God says in: the Acts 15 : 19 – 20

> Wherefore my sentence is ,
> that we trouble not them ,
> which from the Gentiles
> are turned to God :
> but
> that we write unto them ,
> that they abstain from
>
> 1. pollutions of idols
> 2. from fornication
> 3. and from things strangled
> 4. and from blood.

Question: What does that mean " Polutions of Idols "

God says in: Psalms 106 : 35 - 38

But were mingled among the heathen ,
and learned their works ,
and they served their idols :
which were a snare unto them .

Yea,
they sacrificed their sons
and their daughters
unto devils,
and shed innocent blood,
even the blood of their sons
and of their daughters ,
whom they sacrificed unto the idols of Canaan:
and the land was polluted with blood.

Question: What does God want us to do now about this pollution ?

God says in: 1 Corinthians 10 : 14

Wherefore ,
my dearly beloved,
flee from idolatry .

Question: What about if we are invited
to eat in their temples ?

God says in: 1 Corinthians 10 : 28

But if any man say unto you ,
this is offered in sacrifice unto idols,
eat not for his sake that shewed it,
and for conscience sake :

For the earth is the Lord's
and the fullness thereof.

Question: Is it wrong then ,
for us to eat in their temples ?

God says in: 1 Corinthians 8 : 4 – 10

As concerning therefore the eating
of those things that are offered in sacrifice unto idols,
we know that an idol is nothing in the world,
and that there is none other God but one.

For though there be that are called gods,
whether in heaven or in earth,
(as there be gods many, and lords many,)
but to us there is but one God ,
the father, of whom are all things,
and we in him ;
and one Lord Jesus Christ ,
by whom are all things and we by him .

Howbeit there is not in every man that knowledge :
for some with conscience of the idol
unto this hour eat it
as a thing offered unto an idol;
and their conscience being weak is defiled.

But meat commendeth us not to God:
for neither ,
if we eat ,
are we better;
neither ,
if we eat not ,
are we the worse.
But
take heed lest by any means this liberty of yours
become a stumblingblock to them that are weak.

> For if any man see thee
> which hast knowledge
> sit at meat in the idols temple,
> shall not the conscience of him
> which is weak
> be emboldened to eat those things
> which are offered to idols.
> And through thy knowledge
> shall the weak brother perish ,
> for whom Christ died?

Question: Does God still want us, in this age , to be concerned with idols ?

God says in: Colosians 3 : 5 - 6

> Mortify therefore your members
> which are upon the earth ;
>
> fornication ,
> uncleaness ,
> inordinate affection ,
> evil concupiscence , (strong sensual lust)
>
> and covetousness ,
> which is idolatry :
>
> for which things' sake
> the wrath of God cometh
> on the children of disobedience .

Question: How is covetousness connected to Idolatry ?

God says in: Ezekiel 14 : 2 - 6

And the word of the Lord came unto me ,
saying ,
Son of man ,
these men have set up
their idols in their heart,
and put the stumblingblock
of their iniquity before their face:
should I be inquired of
at all by them?

Therefore speak unto them ,
and say unto them ,
Thus saith the Lord God ;

Every man of the house of Israel
that setteth up his idols of his heart ,
and putteth the stumblingblock
of his iniquity before his face,
and cometh to the prophet;

I the Lord will answer him that cometh
according to the multitude of his idols;

That I may take the house of Israel
in their own heart,
because they are
all estranged from me
through their idols.

Therefore
Say unto the house of Israel,
Thus sayeth the Lord God ;
repent ,

and turn yourselves from your idols;
and turn away your faces
from all your abominations.

Authors note: When God talks about
the " idols of your heart ",
it would mean,
anything that you spend more time with
and show more affection for,
than our great God in heaven.

Question: What does God mean ,
to turn away our faces
from all of our abominations ?

God says in: Deuteronomy 7 : 25 – 26

The graven images of their gods
shall ye burn with fire:
thou shalt not desire
the silver
or gold
that is on them,
nor take it unto thee ,
lest thou be snared therin:
for it is an abomination to the Lord thy God.

Neither shalt thou bring
an abomination into thine house,
lest thou be a cursed thing
like it :

but thou shalt utterly detest it ,
and thou shalt utterly abhor it ;
for it is a cursed thing .

Chapter 13

How to stop sinning

The Doctrine of Christ
Ronald F. Peters

Question: Why do people have trouble to stop sinning after they become Christians ?

God says in: Ephesians 6 : 12

For we wrestle not against flesh and blood ,
but
against principalities ,
against powers
against the rulers of the darkness of this world,
against spiritual wickedness in high places.

Question: So when Satans principalities and powers
tempt us to sin
how do we stop it ?

God says in: James 4 : 7

1) Submit yourselves to God

2) resist the devil ,
 and he will flee from you

Question: How do we submit to God
and how do we resist the devil ?

God says in: Romans 6 : 11 – 22

Likewise reckon ye also yourselves
to be dead indeed unto sin,
but alive unto God
through Jesus Christ our Lord .

Let not sin therefore
reign in your mortal body,
that ye should obey it
in the lusts thereof .
Neither yield ye your members
as instruments of unrighteousness unto sin :
but yield yourselves unto God,
as those that are alive from the dead ,
and your members
as instruments of righteousness unto God.

For sin shall not have dominion over you:
for ye are not under the law,
but under grace.

What then ?
shall we sin ,
because we are not under the law,
but under grace ?
God forbid .

Know ye not .
that to whom ye yield yourselves
servants to obey, (servant mode)
his servants ye are
to whom ye obey ;
whether of sin unto death ,

or
of obedience unto righteousness ?

But God be thanked,
that ye were the servants of sin,
but ye have
obeyed from the heart
that form of doctrine
which was delivered you .
Being then made free from sin,
ye became the servants of righteousness .
I speak after the manner of men
because of the infirmity of your flesh :
for as ye have yielded your members
servants to uncleanness
and to iniquity unto iniquity;
even so now yield your members
servants to righteouness unto holiness.

For when ye were the servants of sin,
ye were free from righteousness.

What fruit had ye then
in those things
whereof ye are now ashamed ?
for the end of those things is death .

But now, being made free from sin,
and
become servants to God,
ye have your fruit unto holiness,
and the end "everlasting life".

Question: Are we to understand that
by becoming servants of God,
we are able to stop sinning ?

God says in: 2 Peter 2 : 9

The Lord knoweth how
to deliver the godly out of temptations ,
and to reserve the unjust
unto the day of judgment to be punished .

Question: Did God create
an exact system of steps,
for us to gradually stop sinning ?

God says in: 2 Peter 1 : 3 – 11

According as his divine power
hath given unto us all things
that pertain unto life and godliness ,
through the knowledge of him
that hath called us to glory and virtue :
whereby are given unto us
exceeding great and precious promises:
that by these
ye might be partakers of the divine nature ,

having escaped the corruption
that is in the world through lust
and beside this ,
giving all diligence,
(that means it is not easy,
 you really need to work at it)
add to your :

1. Faith (having unbelief removed)

2. Virtue (resolution to excellence and distinction)

3. Knowledge (clear perception of the truth)

4. Temperance (practice of abstinence & self control)

5 Patience (endurance, suffer without complaint)

6. Godliness (piety , holiness, devout)

7. Brotherly Kindness (affection , friendship)

8. Charity (Christian Love)

For if these things be in you ,
and abound,
they make you
that ye shall neither be barren
nor unfruitful
in the knowledge of our Lord Jesus Christ

But
he that lacketh these things
is blind,
and cannot see afar off,
and hath forgotten
that he was purged from his old sins.

Wherefore the rather ,
brethren,
give diligence
to make your calling
and election
sure:

for if ye do these things,
"ye shall never fall" :
(adding those eight things in order,
guarantees "to never fall"!!)

for so an entrance shall be ministered
unto you abundantly
into the everlasting kingdom of our Lord
and Saviour Jesus Christ

(Note : the 7 things above are in prerequisite order . Eg. You cannot go from knowledge straight to patience. You need temperance first.)

Chapter 14

God's gift of Grace

The Doctrine of Christ
Ronald F. Peters

Question: Can only people that are without sin,
be saved ?

God says in: St . John 3 : 16 -17

For God so loved the world ,
that he gave his only begotten Son,
that whosoever believeth in him
should not perish,
but have everlasting life.
For God sent not his Son into the world
to condemn the world ;
but that the world through him might be saved.

Question: Was God saying
that we need to have faith
to believe in Jesus,
who took our punishment upon himself ,
so that we would not need to be punished ?

God says in: Romans 5 : 1 – 2

Thereforefore being justified by faith,
we have peace with God
through our Lord Jesus Christ.
By whom also
we have access by faith
into his grace
wherein we stand,
and rejoice in hope of the glory of God.

Question: Did God provide an escape from punishment for us, while we were still sinners ?

God says in: God says in Romans 5 : 6 – 11

For when we were yet without strength,
in due time
Christ died for the ungodly.
For scarcely for a righteous man will one die:
yet peradventure for a good man
some would even dare to die.

But God commendeth his love toward us,
in that ,
"while we were yet sinners",
Christ died for us.
Much more then,
being now justified by his blood,
we shall be saved from wrath through him.
For if ,
when we were enemies ,
we were reconciled to God
by the death of his Son,
much more ,
being reconciled ,
we shall be saved by his life.
And not only so ,
but we also joy in God through out Lord Jesus Christ ,
by whom we have now received the atonement.

Question: But it doesn't say that a person
needs to get rid of all their sin first,
in order to get saved ?
Why does God accept us
when we are still sinners ?

God says in: Ephesians 2 : 1 – 9

And you
hath he quickened ,
who were dead in trespasses and sins;

Wherein in time past
ye walked according to the course of this world
according to the prince of the power of the air,
the spirit that now worketh
in the children of disobedience:

Among whom also
we all had our conversation in times past
in the lusts of our flesh,
fulfilling the desires of the flesh
and of the mind;
and were by nature the children of wrath,
even as others.

But God ,
who is rich in mercy,
for his great love wherewith he loved us ,
even when we were dead in sins,
hath quickened us together with Christ,
(by grace ye are saved)

And hath raised us up together ,
and made us sit together
in heavenly places in Christ Jesus:
That in the ages to come

he might shew the exceeding riches of his grace
in his kindness toward us
through Christ Jesus .

For by grace are ye saved through faith;
and that not of yourselves:
it is the gift of God:
Not of works,
lest any man should boast.

Authors note: In the old Testament we had the laws,
which everyone disobeyed.
The Bible says
all have sinned
and come short of the glory of God.

Because of the system of the Laws
which could not work,
God created an escape for us.
God sent his Son Jesus down to earth ,
to die for us ,
taking all our sin upon himself,
and then rose again to life.

If we believe

that he took our punishment upon himself ,
and accept that he is our Saviour ,
we now are free by grace,
not by works ,
and we will never be condemned ,
to eternal punishment
in the lake of fire.

Question: How did St. Paul describe this grace ?

God says in: Galatians 2 : 16 – 21

> Knowing that a man is not justified
> by the works of the law,
> but by the faith of Jesus Christ,
> even we have believed in Jesus Christ,
> that we might be justified by the faith of Christ,
> and not by the works of the law:
> for by the works of the law
> shall no flesh be justified.
> But if,
> while we seek to be justified by Christ
> we ourselves also are found sinners,
> is therefore Christ the minister of sin ?
> God forbid.
> For if I build again
> the things which I destroyed,
> I make myself a transgressor.
> For I through the law
> am dead to the law,
> that I might live unto God.
> I am crucified with Christ:
> nevertheless I live;
> yet not I ,
> but Christ liveth in me:
> and the life which I now live in the flesh
> I live by the faith of the Son of God,
> who loved me,
> and gave himself for me.
> I do not frustrate the grace of God,
> for if righteousness come by the law,
> then Christ is dead in vain.

Question: Can we really be sure of this grace ?

God says in: Galatians 5 : 1

Stand fast therefore in the liberty
wherewith Christ has made us free,
and be not entangled again
with the yoke of bondage.

Question: Now that we have Gods grace,
what does God expect of us ?

God says in: Galatians 6 : 7 – 10

Be not deceived ;
God is not mocked:
for whatsoever a man soweth ,
that shall he also reap.
For he that soweth to his flesh
shall of the flesh reap corruption;
but he that soweth to the Spirit
shall of the Spirit reap life everlasting.
And let us not be weary in well doing:
for in due season we shall reap,
if we faint not.
As we have therefore opportunity,
let us do good unto all men,
especially unto them
who are of the household of faith.

Chapter 15

Darkness and Light

The Doctrine of Christ
Ronald F. Peters

Question: To what is God referring to
when he talks about darkness and light ?

God says in: Proverbs 4 : 18 - 19

But the path of the just
is as the shining light ,
that shineth more and more
unto the perfect day.
The way of the wicked
is as darkness:
they know not
at what they stumble .

Question: Because we think of ourselves
in a modern age,
what if some people say that certain sins
are alright now ?

God says in: Isaiah 5 : 20

Woe unto them that call evil good,
and good evil ;
that put darkness for light ,
and light for darkness ;
that put bitter for sweet ,
and sweet for bitter !

Question: What causes us to get into darkness ?

God says in: St Matthew 6 : 22 - 23

The light of the body is the eye:
If therefore thine eye be single (good or sound)
thy whole body shall be full of light .
But if thine eye be evil,
thy whole body shall be full of darkness.

If therefore the light that is in thee be darkness,
How great is that darkness !

Question: How do we get light
instead of darkness ?

God says in: St John 1 : 4 – 5

In him was life;
and the life was the light of men
and the light shineth in darkness;
and the darkness comprehended it not .

Question: Are there any consequences
for being full of darkness ?

God says in: St John 3 : 16 - 21

For God so loved the world ,
that he gave his only begotten Son ,
that whosoever believeth in him should not perish ,
but have everlasting life.
For
God sent not his Son into the world
to condemn the world ;
but that the world through him
might be saved.

He that believeth on him
is not condemned :
but he that believeth not
is condemned already ,
because
he hath not believed in the name
of the only begotten Son of God .

Note this: And this is the condemnation ,

that light is come into the world,
and men loved darkness rather than light ,
because their deeds were evil .
For every one that doeth evil
hateth the light ,
neither cometh to the light ,
lest his deeds should be reproved .
But he that doeth truth ,
cometh to the light ,
that his deeds may be made manifest,
that they are wrought in God.

Question: How do we avoid this darkness
and the condemnation ?

God says in: St John 8 : 12

Then spake Jesus again unto them saying ,
I am the light of the world :
he that followeth me
shall not walk in darkness,
but shall have the light of life.

Question: Is following Jesus
part of coming to the light ?

God says in: St John 12 : 35 – 36

Then Jesus said unto them ,
yet a little while is the light with you ,
walk while ye have the light ,
lest darkness come upon you:
for he that walketh in darkness
knoweth not whither he goeth .

While ye have light ,
believe in the light ,
that ye may be the children of light .

These things spake Jesus ,
and departed ,
and did hide himself from them .

Question: How do we get out of darkness ?

God says in: St John 12 : 46

I am come a light into the world ,
that whosoever believeth on me
should not abide in darkness .

Question: How exactly does this process work turning from darkness to light ?

God says in: The Acts 26 : 18

To open their eyes ,
and
turn them from darkness to light ,
and
from the power of Satan
unto God ,
that they may receive forgivness of sins,
and inheritance among them which are sanctified
by faith that is in me .

Question: What does God say to people that are still in darkness ?

God says in: Ephesians 5 : 6 - 13

Let no man deceive you
with vain words :
for because of these things
cometh the wrath of God
upon the children of disobedience .

Be not ye therefore
partakers with them .
For ye were sometimes darkness,
But now are ye light in the Lord :
Walk as children of light :
(for the fruit of the Spirit is in all
goodness and righteousness and truth ;)
proving what is acceptable unto the Lord.

And have no fellowship
with the unfruitful works of darkness ,
but rather reprove them.
For

Note this: it is a shame
even to speak of those things
which are done of them in secret .

But all things that are reproved
are made manifest by the light :
for whatsoever doth make manifest is light .

Question: Why do we need Christ
to remove our darkness
by giving us light ?

God says in: Ephesians 6 : 12

For we wrestle not against flesh and blood ,
but
against principalities ,
against powers ,
against the rulers of the darkness of this world ,
against spiritual wickedness in high places .

Question: How does God deliver us from these
principalities and powers ?

God says in: Colossians 1 : 12 – 14

Giving thanks unto the Father ,
which hath made us meet to be partakers
of the inheritance
of the saints in light :
who hath delivered us
from the power of darkness ,
and
hath translated us into the kingdom
of his dear Son:
in whom we have redemption through his blood ,
even the forgiveness of sins .

Authors note: In Volume One , Chapter 13 we read,
how the fire devouring
before King Jesus will burn all those,
not able to come to the light,
because of their darkness of sin.

Chapter 16

The Covenants

The Doctrine of Christ
Ronald F. Peters

Question: What is Abrahams Covenant all about ?

God says in: Genesis 17 : 1 – 14

And when Abram was ninety years old and nine , (99)
the Lord appeared to Abram,
and said unto him ,

I am the Almighty God ;
walk before me ,
and be thou perfect.
And I will make my covenant
between me and thee,

1) and will multiply thee exceedingly.
And Abram fell on his face :
and God talked with him ,
saying ,
as for me ,
behold,
my covenant is with thee,

2) and thou shalt be a father of many nations .
Neither shall thy name any more be called Abram ,
but thy name shall be Abraham ;
for a father of many nations
have I made thee.

And I will make thee exceeding fruitful ,
and I will make nations of thee,
and kings shall come out of thee.
And I will establish my covenant
between me and thee and thy seed after thee
in their generations for an everlasting covenant,

3) to be a God unto thee,
and to thy seed after thee.
and I will give unto thee ,
and to thy seed after thee,
the land wherein thou art a stranger ,
all the land of Canaan ,
for and everlasting possession;
for I will be their God .

And God said unto Abraham ,
thou shalt keep my covenant therefore,
thou,
and thy seed after thee in their generations .

4) This is my covenant ,
which ye shall keep,
between me and you and thy seed after thee;
every man child among you shall be circumcised.

And ye shall circumcise the flesh of your foreskin;
and it shall be a token of the covenant
betwixt me and you .

And he that is eight days old
shall be circumcised among you ,
every man child in your generations ,
he that is born in the house ,
or bought with money of any stranger ,
which is not of thy seed .

He that is born in thy house,
and he that is bought with thy money ,
must needs be circumcised :
and my covenant shall be in your flesh
for an everlasting covenant .

Ronald F. Peters Questions

And the uncircumcised man child
whose flesh of his foreskin
is not circumcised ,
that soul shall be cut off from his people;
he hath broken my covenant .

Question: Did God add anything else to this Covenant ?

God says in: Exodus 19 : 1 – 6

In the third month ,
when the children of Israel were gone forth
out of the land of Egypt
the same day came they into the wilderness of Sinai.

For they were departed from Rephidim,
and were come to the desert of Sinai,
and had pitched in the wilderness ;
and there Israel camped before the mount.

And Moses went up unto God,
and the Lord called unto him
out of the mountain,
saying ,
thus shalt thou say to the house of Jacob,
and tell the children of Israel;

ye have seen what I did unto the Egyptians ,
and how I bare you on eagles' wings,
and brought you unto myself.

Now therefore ,
if ye will
1) obey my voice indeed ,
2) and keep my covenant ,

then ye shall be
a peculiar treasure unto me
above all people :
for all the earth is mine :

and ye shall be unto me
a kingdom of priests,
and an holy nation .

These are the words
which thou shalt speak
unto the children of Israel .

Question: Was anything else put into the covenant ?

God says in: Exodus 31 : 12 - 18

And the Lord spake unto Moses .
saying,
speak thou also unto the children of Israel ,

saying ,
verily my Sabbaths ye shall keep:
for it is a sign between me and you
throughout your generations ,
that ye may know that I am the Lord
that doth sanctify you.

Ye shall keep the Sabbath therefore;
for it is holy unto you :
Everyone that defileth it
shall surely be put to death :
for whosoever doeth any work therein,
that soul shall be cut off from among his people.

Six days may work be done;
but in the seventh is the Sabbath of rest,
holy to the Lord :
whosoever doeth any work in the Sabbath day,
he shall surely be put to death.

Wherefore the children of Israel shall keep the Sabbath,
to observe the Sabbath throughout their generations,
for a " perpetual covenant " .

It is a sign between
me and the children of Israel for ever :
for in six days the Lord made heaven and earth ,
and on the seventh day he rested,
and was refreshed .

And he gave unto Moses,
when he had made an end
of communing with him upon Mount Sinai,
two tables of testimony,
tables of stone,
written with the finger of God.

Question: Did God keep his covenant
with Abraham and his children ?

God says in: Exodus 2 : 23 - 24

And it came to pass in process of time ,
That the king of Egypt died:
And the children of Israel sighed
by reason of the bondage ,
and they cried ,
and their cry came up unto God
by reason of the bondage.

And God heard their groaning ,
and God remembered his covenant with Abraham,
with Isaac and with Jacob . (Israel – Genesis 32: 28)

Question: For how many more generations
did God keep this covenant ?

God says in: Deuteronomy 5 : 3

The Lord made not this covenant
with our fathers,
but with us ,
even us ,
who are all of us here
alive this day

Question: Did God really mean all the people that are alive today ?

God says in: The Acts 3 : 25

Ye are the children of the prophets
and of the covenant
which God made with our fathers,
saying unto Abraham ,
and in thy seed
shall all the kindreds of the earth
be blessed .

Question: When God added the "Ten Commandments" to the covenant did he also add another "benefit" ?

God says in: Deuteronomy 6 : 17 – 19

Ye shall diligently keep the commandments
of the Lord your God ,
and his testimonies,
and his statutes ,
which he hath commanded thee.

And thou shalt do that
which is right and good
in the sight of the Lord:
that it may be well with thee,

and that thou mayest go in
and possess the good land
which the Lord sware unto thy fathers ,

to cast out all thine enemies
from before thee,
as the Lord hath spoken .

Question: Since we are not decendents of Abraham , did God ever make a covenant for us Gentiles ?

God says in: Galatians 3 : 14

That the blessings of Abraham
might come on the Gentiles
through Jesus Christ;
that we might receive
the promise of the Spirit through faith .

Question: What changed in this second covenant ?

God says in: Hebrews 8 : 6 - 13

But now he hath obtained
a more excellent ministry,
by how much also
he is the mediator
of a better covenant,
which was established
upon better promises .

For if
that first covenant had been faultless ,
then should no place have been sought
for the second .

for finding fault with them ,
he saith ,
behold ,
the days come ,
saith the Lord,
when I will make a new covenant
with the house of Israel
and with the house of Judah :

not according to the covenant
that I made with their fathers
in the day
when I took them by the hand
to lead them out of the land of Egypt;

because they continued not
in my covenant ,
and I regarded them not,
saith the Lord.

      For
      this is the covenant
      that I will make
      with the house of Israel after those days ,
      saith the Lord ;

1. I will put my laws into their mind,
   and
   write them in their hearts:

2. and I will be to them a God ,
   and
   they shall be to me a people :

      and

3. they shall not teach
   every man his neighbour,
   and every man his brother,
   saying ,
   know the Lord:
   for all shall know me,
   from the least to the greatest.

4. For I will be merciful
   to their unrighteousness,
   and their sins
   and their iniquities
   will I remember no more .

      In that he saith ,
      a new covenant ,
      he hath made the first old.

      Now that which decayeth and waxeth old
      is ready to vanish away.

Question: Since the first covenant was accepted
and confirmed by circumcision of the flesh ,
how is the second covenant confirmed ?

God says in: Colossians 2 : 10 - 14

And ye are complete in him
which is the head
of all principality
and power:
in whom also ye are circumcised
with the circumcision made without hands,
putting off the body of the sins of the flesh

by the circumcision of Christ :
" buried with him in baptism " ,

wherein also ye are risen with him
through the faith of the operation of God ,
who hath raised him from the dead.
And you,
being dead in your sins
and the uncircumcision of your flesh ,

hath he quickened together with him,
having forgiven you all trespasses ;
blotting out the handwriting
of ordinances that was against us,
which was contrary to us,
and took it out of the way ,
nailing it to his cross.

Question: If we are buried in baptism with Christ
are we still heirs of Abrahams covenant
as well as the new covenant ?

God says in: Galatians 3 : 29

And if
ye be Christ's ,
then are ye Abrahams seed ,
and heirs according to the promise .

Question: Because we are now of Abrahams seed ,
can we say that we are of the circumcision ?

God says in: Philippians 3 : 3

For we are the circumcision ,
which worship God in the spirit ,
and rejoice in Christ Jesus ,
and have no confidence in the flesh .

The old Covenant	The new Covenant
Benefits	Benefits
1. multiply Abraham exceedingly	1. all the blessings of Abraham
2. father of many nations	2. God's laws will be in our minds
3. would be a God unto him and his seed after him	3. God's laws in our hearts
	4. remembered our sins no more
4. possess the good land	5. will be unto us a God
5. cast out all his enemies from before him	6. we shall be God's people
6. sin removed by animal blood	7. eternal Salvation and heaven
	8. adopted children of God
	9. the blood of Jesus as our atonement for sin
	10. receive the Holy Spirit
Conditions	Conditions
1. all 8 days old males to be circumcized	1. Confess our sins and repent
2. obey God's voice	2. believe on the Lord Jesus Christ
3. keep God's covenant	3. Buried with Christ in Baptism
4. keep the Sabbath	4. put on Christ
5. keep the ten Commandments	5. become servants and follow him
	6. obey God's voice

Chapter 17

The Priesthood Of Jesus Christ

The Doctrine of Christ
Ronald F. Peters

Question: What was involved with the priesthood in the beginning ?

God says in: Exodus 28 : 1 – 8

And take thou unto thee
Aaron thy brother ,
and his sons with him ,
from among the children of Israel,
that he may minister unto me
in the priest's office,
even Aaron ,
Nadab, and Abihu, Eleazar and Ithamar,
Aaron's sons.
and thou shalt make holy garments
for Aaron thy brother ,
for glory and for beauty .

And thou shalt speak unto all
that are wise hearted,
whom I have filled with the "Spirit of Wisdom" ,
that they may make Aaron's garments
to consecrate him ,
that he may minister unto me
in the priests office.

And these are the garments
which they shall make;

a breastplate,
and an ephod ,
and a robe,
and a broidered coat,
a mitre,
and a girdle :
And they shall make holy garments

for Aaron thy brother, and his sons,
that he may minister unto me
in the priests office.

And they shall take

gold,
and blue,
and purple,
and scarlet,
and fine linen.

And they shall make the ephod

of gold ,
of blue,
and of purple,
of scarlet,
and of fine twined linen ,
with cunning work.. (skillfully embroidered)

It shall have the two shoulders-pieces thereof
joined at the two edges thereof;
and so it shall be joined together .

Question: What were some of their immediate duties
to make them holy
to minister unto the Lord
in the Priest's office ?

God says in: Exodus 29 : 1 - 7

And this is the thing
that thou shalt do unto them
to hallow them ,
to minister unto me
in the priest's office :

Take one young bullock,
and two rams without blemish ,
and unleavened bread ,
and cakes unleavened tempered with oil ,
and wafers unleavened anointed with oil :
of wheaten flour shalt thou make them .
And thou shalt put them into one basket ,
and bring them in the basket ,
with the bullock and the two rams.

And Aaron and his sons thou shalt bring
unto the door of the tabernacle of the congregation,
and shalt wash them with water.

And thou shalt take the garments ,
and put upon Aaron the coat ,
and the robe of the ephod,
and the ephod,
and the breastplate ,
and gird him with the curious girdle of the ephod:
and thou shalt put the mitre upon his head,
and put the holy crown upon the mitre .

Then shalt thou take the anointing oil ,
and pour it upon his head,
and anoint him.

Question: What about the bullock and the Ram ?

God says in: Exodus 29 : 11 - 18

And thou shalt kill the bullock before the Lord,
by the door of the tabernacle of the congregation.
and thou shalt take of the blood of the bullock ,
and put it upon the horns of the alter with thy finger,
and pour all the blood beside the bottom of the altar.

And thou shalt take all the fat
that covereth the inwards,
and the caul that is above the liver,
and the two kidneys,
and the fat that is upon them ,
and burn them upon the altar.

But the flesh of the bullock ,
and his skin ,
and his dung ,
shalt thou burn with fire without the camp:
it is a sin offering .
Thou shalt also take one ram:
and Aaron and his sons
shall put their hands upon the head of the ram.

And thou shalt slay the ram,
and thou shalt take his blood ,
and sprinkle it round about the altar .
and thou shalt cut the ram in pieces ,
and wash the inwards of him ,
and his legs, and put them unto his pieces,
and unto his head.

And thou shalt burn
the whole ram upon the altar :
it is a burnt offering unto the Lord:

it is a sweet savour ,
an offering made by fire unto the Lord.

Question: Were Aaron and his sons the first priests ?

God says in: Genesis 14 : 14 - 20

And when Abram heard (430 years before Moses and Aaron)
that his brother was taken captive ,
he armed his trained servants,
born in his own house,
three hundred and eighteen, (That's quite a house-318 trained servants)
and pursued them unto Dan.

And he divided himself against them ,
he and his servants,
by night ,
and smote them ,
and pursued them unto Hobah,
which is on the left hand of Damascus .
(That's north in Syria)

And he brought back all the goods,
and also brought again his brother Lot ,
and his goods,
and the women also ,
and the people .

And the King of Sodom went out to meet him
after his return
from the slaughter of Chedorlaomer ,
and of the kings that were with him ,
at the valley of Shaveh,
which is the kings dale.

And " Melchizedek " King of Salem
brought forth bread and wine:
and he was the priest

of the most high God.
and he blessed him ,

and said,

"Blessed be Abram of the most high God ,
possessor of heaven and earth :
and blessed be the most high God,
which hath delivered thine enemies
into thy hand."

And he gave him tithes of all .

(Abram gave 10 % to King Melchizedek)

Question: Why didn't " Melchizedec " need to go through the purification rituals like Aaron and his sons ?

God says in: Hebrews 5 : 1 – 11

For every High priest
taken from among men
is ordained for men
in things pertaining to God ,
that he may offer both gifts and sacrifices for sins:
who can have compassion on the ignorant,
and on them that are out of the way;
for that he himself
also is compassed with infirmity.

And by reason hereof he ought ,
as for the people,
so also for himself,
to offer for sins.
And no man taketh this honour unto himself,
but he that is called of God,
as was Aaron .

So also Christ glorified not himself
to be made an high priest;

but he that said unto him ,
thou art my Son ,
today have I begotten thee.

As he saith also in another place,
Thou art a priest forever
after the order of " Melchisedec " .

Who in the days of his flesh ,
when he had offered up prayers
and supplications with strong crying and tears

unto him that was able to save him from death ,
and was heard in that he feared;

though he were a Son ,
yet learned he obedience
by the things which he suffered;
and being made perfect
he became the author of eternal salvation
unto all them that obey him;

Called of God an high priest
after the order of " Melchisedec ".

of whom we have many things to say,
and hard to be uttered,
seeing ye are dull of hearing .

Question: But what made " Melchisedec " the high priest so special, that God wanted Jesus to be of his order of high priests ?

God says in: Hebrews 7 : 1 - 28

For this " Melchisedec ",
king of Salem,
priest of the most high God,
who met Abraham returning
from the slaughter of the kings,
and blessed him ;

to whom also Abraham gave a tenth part of all ;
first being by interpretation
King of Righteousness ,
and after that also
King of Salem,
which is
King of Peace;

without father ,
without mother,
without descent ,
having neither beginning of days,
nor end of life;
but made like unto the Son of God ;
abideth a priest continually .

Now consider how great this man was,
unto whom even the patriarch Abraham
gave the tenth of the spoils.

And verily they that are of the sons of Levi,
who receive the office of the priesthood,
have a commandment to take tithes of the people
according to the law,

that is ,
of their brethren ,
though they come out of the loins of Abraham:

but
he whose descent is not counted from them
received tithes of Abraham ,
and blessed him that had the promises.

And without all contradiction
the less is blessed of the better.

And here (down here on earth)
men that die, receive tithes;
but
there he receiveth them,
of whom it is witnessed that he liveth .

And as I may so say,
Levi also ,
who receiveth tithes ,
payed tithes in Abraham.

For he was yet in the loins of his father, (Levi)
when " Melchisedec " met him . (Abraham)

If therefore perfection
were by the Levitical priesthood ,
(for under it the people received the law ,)
what further need was there
that another priest should rise
after the order of Melchisedec ,
and not be called after the order of Aaron ?

For the Priesthood being changed,
there is made of necessity a change also of the law.

For he of whom these things are spoken

pertaineth to another tribe,
of which no man gave attendance at the altar.

For it is evident
that our Lord sprang out of Juda ,
of which tribe Moses spake nothing
concerning priesthood.
And it is yet far more evident :
for that after the similitude of Melchisedec
there ariseth another priest,
who is made,
not after the law of a carnal commandment ,
but after the power of an endless life.

For he testifieth ,
thou art a priest forever
after the order of Melchisedec .

For there is verily a disannulling
of the commandment going before
for the weakness and unprofitableness thereof.

For the law made nothing perfect,
but the bringing in of a better hope did ;
by the which we draw nigh unto God.

And inasmuch
as not without an oath
he was made priest :
(for those priests were made without an oath ;
but this with an oath
by him that said unto him,
the Lord sware and will not repent,
"thou are a priest forever
after the order of Melchisedec":) ,

By so much was Jesus made a surety
of a better testament .
And they truly were many priests,
because they were not suffered to continue
by reason of death :
but this man ,
because he continueth ever,
hath an unchangeable priesthood.

Wherefore he is able also to save them
to the uttermost
that come unto God by him,
seeing he ever liveth to make intercession
for them .

For such an high priest became us ,
who is holy ,
harmless ,
undefiled ,
separate from sinners,
and made higher than the heavens;
who needeth not daily ,
as those high priests,
to offer up sacrifice,
first for his own sins,
and then for the people's :
for this he did once,
when he offered up himself.

For the law maketh men high priests
which have infirmity ;
but the word of the oath ,
which was since the law,
maketh the Son,
who is consecrated for evermore.

Question: What does Jesus do now ,
up in heaven ,
as our High Priest ?

God says in: Hebrews 8 : 1 - 6

Now of the things which we have spoken
This is the sum :

We have such an high priest,
who is set on the right hand of the throne
of the Majesty in the heavens;
A minister of the sanctuary,
and of the true tabernacle,
which the Lord pitched ,
and not man .
For every high priest is ordained
to offer gifts and sacrifices :
Wherefore it is of necessity
that this man
have somewhat also to offer .

For if he were on earth,
he should not be a priest,
seeing that there are priests
that offer gifts
according to the law :

who serve unto the example and shadow
of heavenly things ,
as Moses was admonished of God
when he was about to make the tabernacle :
for ,
See,
saith he ,
that thou make all things

according to the pattern shewed to thee
in the mount .

But now hath he obtained
a more excellent ministry ,
by how much also he is the mediator
of a better covenant ,
which was established
upon better promises .

Chapter 18

King Jesus' final instruction

The Doctrine of Christ
Ronald F. Peters

Question: What did Saint Matthew write
about the last words of Jesus
as he (King Jesus) was leaving planet earth ?

God says in: St. Matthew 28 : 18 – 20

And Jesus came
and spake unto them ,
saying ,

All power is given unto me
in heaven and in earth

Go ye therefore , (because of the power)
and teach all nations,

baptizing them
in the name
1. of the Father ,
2. and of the Son,
3. and of the Holy Ghost :

Teaching them to observe
all things whatsoever
I have commanded you:

and,
lo,
I am with you always,
even unto the end of the world.
Amen.

Question: What did Saint Mark write about the last words of King Jesus as he was leaving earth ?

God says in: St Mark 16 : 15 - 20

And he said unto them,
go ye into all the world,
and preach the gospel
to every creature.

He that

1. believeth
2. and is baptized

shall be saved ;

but
he that believeth not
shall be damned.

And these signs shall follow them that believe;

1. in my name shall they cast out devils;
2. the shall speak with new tongues;
3. they shall take up serpents;
4. and if they drink any deadly thing, it shall not hurt them;
5. they shall lay hands on the sick, and they shall recover.

So then, after the Lord had spoken unto them,
he was received up into heaven,
and sat on the right hand of God.

And they went forth ,
and preached every where ,
the Lord working with them,

and confirming the word with signs following .

Amen .

Question: What did Saint Luke write
about the last words of King Jesus
as he was leaving earth ?

God says in: St. Luke 24 : 45 – 53

Then opened he their understanding ,
that they might understand the scriptures ,
and said unto them,

thus it is written,
and thus it behoved Christ to suffer,
and to rise from the dead the third day:

and that
1. repentance
2. and remission of sins (water baptism)

should be preached
in his name
among all nations,
beginning at Jerusalem.

And ye are witnesses of these things .
And ,
behold,
I send the promise of my father upon you: (the Holy Spirit)

but tarry ye in the city of Jerusalem,
until ye be endued with power from on high.

And he led them out as far as to Bethany,
and he lifted up his hands,
and blessed them.

And it came to pass,
while he blessed them,

he was parted from them,
and carried up into heaven.

And they worshipped him,
and returned to Jerusalem with great joy;
and were continually in the temple,
praising and blessing God .

Amen.

Question: What did Saint John write about the last words of King Jesus as he was leaving earth ?

God says in: St. John 20 : 21 – 23

Then said Jesus to them again ,
Peace be unto you:
As my Father hath sent me,
Even so send I you.

And when he had said this ,
He breathed on them , (a week before with a different group)
and saith unto them ,
receive ye the Holy Ghost:

1. whose soever sins ye remit, (water baptism) they are remitted unto them;

    and whose soever sins ye retain,
    they are retained.

Question: What did Saint Paul write about the last words of King Jesus as he was leaving earth ?

God says in: The Acts 1 : 4 - 12

And ,
being assembled together with them,
commanded them that they should not
depart from Jerusalem ,
but wait, for the promise of the Father,
which, he saith,
ye have heard of me.
for John truly baptized with water;
but ye shall be baptized
with the Holy Ghost
not many days hence.
When they therefore were come together ,
they asked of him saying,
Lord, wilt thou at this time restore again
the kingdom to Israel ?
and he said unto them ,
it is not for you to know the times or the seasons,
which the Father hath put in his own power.

But
ye shall receive power,
after that the Holy Ghost is come upon you:
and ye shall be witnesses unto me
both in Jerusalem,
and in all Judaea,
and in Samaria ,
and unto the uttermost part of the earth .

And when he had spoken these things,
while they beheld,

he was taken up;

and a cloud received him out of their sight .

and while they looked stedfastly toward heaven as he went up,

behold, two men stood by them in white apparel ;

which also said, ye men of Galilee,

why stand ye gazing up into heaven ?

This same Jesus, which is taken up from you into heaven,

shall so come in like manner as ye have seen him go into heaven.

Then returned they unto Jerusalem from the mount called Olivet,

which is from Jerusalem , a Sabbath day's journey.

Question: This is "the summary"
of all these things
that King Jesus instructed us to do
as he rose up to heaven…

Because I've got all the power now ,
to share with you ,

1. you can be endued from on high
   with this power
   by receiving the Holy Ghost
2. go to all the nations of the world
3. teach them about the gospel and repentance
4. baptize them for the remission of sins
5. and you will be able to :
a. cast out devils using my name
b. you will be able to speak with new tongues
c. you could take up serpents
d. you could drink anything deadly and it won't hurt you
e. you can lay hands on the sick and they will recover.

Finally, don't forget
that I will be with you
all the time,
even to the end of the world.

Authors footnote:

Of all the thousands of things
King Jesus could have said,
as he was about to be lifted off of this planet
and go back to his throne in heaven,
knowing that his words
would need to suffice for generations to come ,
and that these generations
would be up to and at least 2000 years later,
King Jesus thoughtfully chose to leave us
with the five basic instructions .

Not wishing to overload us
with a great burden of obligation,
King Jesus clearly confined his message
to all future peoples :

to   1. receive the power available to them,
and 2. get out there
and 3. teach the simple message of repentance
and 4. baptize them for the remission of sins,
and 5. Confirm that he is real
    by casting out devils
    and healing the sick.

Chapter 19

God has never been Democratic

The Doctrine of Christ
Ronald F. Peters

Question: At no time in history
has God ever suggested
that the people should vote on an issue.
God has always ruled by himself,
without counselors or advice.
Initially, there were judges over Israel,
such as Moses, Joshua, and Samuel.
But eventually, the people wanted to have
a King over them,
just like all of the heathen nations.

How did God react to that?

God says in: 1 Samuel 8 : 1 - 22

And it came to pass,
when Samuel was old,
that he made his sons judges over Israel.

Now the name of his firstborn was Joel;
and the name of his second, Abiah;
they were judges in Beersheba.

And his sons walked not in his ways,
but turned aside after lucre, (Lucre is money)
and took bribes, and perverted judgment.

Then all the elders of Israel
gathered themselves together,
and came to Samuel unto Ramath,
and said unto him,

Behold, thou art old,
and thy sons walk not in thy ways :
now make us a King, to judge us
like all the nations.

But the thing displeased Samuel,

when they said ,
give us a King to judge us .

And Samuel prayed unto the Lord.

And the Lord said unto Samuel ,
Hearken unto the voice of the people
in all that they say unto thee :
for they have not rejected thee ,
but they have rejected me,
that I should not reign over them.

According to all the works which they have done
since the day that I brought them up out of Egypt
even unto this day ,
wherewith they have forsaken me,
and served other gods,
so do they also unto thee.

Now therefore
hearken unto their voice:
howbeit yet protest solemnly unto them ,
and shew them the manner of the King
that shall reign over them.

And Samuel told all the words of the Lord
unto the people that asked of him a King.

And he said ,
This will be the manner of the King
that shall reign over you:
He will take your sons,
and appoint them for himself ,
for his chariots,
and to be his horsemen ;
and some shall run before his chariots.
And he will appoint him captains over thousands ,

and captains of fifties;
and will set them to ear his ground,
and reap his harvest
and to make his instruments of war ,
and instruments of his chariots.
And he will take your daughters
to be confectionaries ,
and to be cooks,
and to be bakers.
And he will take your fields ,
and your vineyards ,
and your oliveyards ,
even the best of them ,
and give them to his servants.
And he will take the tenth of your seed ,
and of your vineyards,
and give to his officers ,
and to his servants.

And he will take your menservants ,
and your maidservants,
and your goodliest young men ,
and your asses ,
and put them to his work.

He will take the tenth of your sheep :
and ye shall be his servants.

And ye shall cry out in that day
because of your King
which ye shall have chosen you;
and the Lord will not hear you,
in that day.

Nevertheless
the people refused to obey

the voice of Samuel;
and they said,

Nay ;
but we will have a king over us;
that we may be like all the nations;
and that our king may judge us,
and go out before us ,
and fight our battles.

And Samuel heard all the words of the people ,
and he rehearsed them in the ears of the Lord .

And the Lord said to Samuel,
Hearken unto their voice,
and make them a king.

And Samuel said unto the men of Israel ,
go ye every man unto his city .

Question: How did Samuel find them a King ?

God says in: 1 Samuel 9 : 1 - 27

Now there was a man of Benjamin,
whose name was Kish,

the son of Abiel,
the son of Zehor,
the son of Bechorath ,
the son of Aphiah,
a Benjamite,
a mighty man of power.

And he had a son ,
whose name was Saul,
a choice young man ,
and a goodly:

and there was not among the children of Israel
a goodlier person than he:
from his shoulders and upward
he was higher than any of the people

And the asses of Kish
Sauls father were lost .

And Kish said to Saul his son,
Take now one of the servants with thee ,
and arise, go seek the asses.

And he passed through Mount Ephraim ,
and passed through the land of Shalisha,
but they found them not.
:
And he passed athrough the land of Shalim,
and there they were not:
and he passed through the land of the Benjamites,

but they found them not.
And when they were come to the land of Zuph,
Saul said to his servant that was with him ,
Come, and let us return;
lest my father leave caring for the asses ,
and take thought for us.

And he said unto him , (The servant said unto Saul)
behold now ,
there is in this city a man of God,
and he is an honorable man ;
all that he saith
cometh surely to pass :
now let us go thither;
peradventure he can show us
our way that we should go .

Then said Saul to his Servant ,
but,
behold,
if we go,
what shall we bring the man?
For the bread is spent in our vessels,
and there is not a present
to bring to the man of God:
what have we?

And the servant answered Saul again ,
and said,
Behold,
I have here at hand
the fourth part of a shekel of silver:
that will I give to the man of God,
to tell our way.

(before time in Israel ,
when a man went to enquire of God,

Thus he spake,
Come, and let us go to the seer:
for he that is now called a Prophet
was beforetime called a seer.)

Then said Saul to his servant .
well said;
come , let us go.

So they went unto the city
where the man of God was.

And as they went up the hill to the city,
they found young maidens
going out to draw water,
and said unto them ,
is the seer here ?

And they answered them ,

(The young maidens answered)
and said , he is before you:
make haste now,
for he came to day to the city ;
for there is a sacrifice of the people to day
in the high place:

as soon as ye be come into the city ,
ye shall straightway find him,
before he go up to the high place to eat:
for the people will not eat until he come,
because he doth bless the sacrifice ;
and afterwards they eat that be bidden.

Now therefore get you up ;
for about this time ye shall find him.

And they went up into the city :
And when they were come into the city,
Behold ,
Samuel came out against them ,
for to go up to the high place.

Now the Lord had told Samuel
in his ear a day before Saul came,
saying , tomorrow about this time
I will send thee a man
out of the land of Benjamin,
and thou shalt anoint him to be captain
over my people Israel,
that he may save my people
out of the hand of the Philistines:
For I have looked upon my people,
because their cry is come unto me.

And when Samuel saw Saul,
The Lord said unto him ,
Behold the man whom I spake to thee of !
This same shall reign over my people.
Then Saul drew near to Samuel in the gate,
and said ,
Tell me,
I pray thee,
where the seer's house is.

And Samuel answered Saul,
and said ,
I am the seer :
Go up before me unto the high place;
for ye shall eat with me to day,
and tomorrow I will let thee go ,
and tell thee all that is in thine heart .

And as for thine asses that were lost three days ago ,
set not thy mind on them;
for they are found.
And on whom is all the desire of Israel ?
Is it not on thee,
and on all thy father's house ?

And Saul answered and said,
am not I a Benjamite ,
of the smallest of the tribes of Israel ?
and my family
the least of all the families of the tribe of Benjamin ?
wherefore then speakest thou so to me ?
And Samuel took Saul and his servant,
and brought them into his parlour,
and made them sit in the chiefest place
among them that were bidden,
which were about thirty persons.

And
Samuel said unto the cook,
bring a portion which I gave thee,
of which I said unto thee,
set it by thee.

And the cook took up the shoulder,
and that which was upon it
and set it before Saul.

And Samuel said,
behold that which is left !
set it before thee, and eat :
for unto this time
hath it been kept for thee
since I said,
I have invited the people.
So Saul did eat with Samuel that day.

And when they were come down
from the high place into the city,
Samuel communed with Saul
upon the top of the house.

And they rose early;
and it came to pass about the spring of the day,
that Samuel called Saul
to the top of the house ,
saying, up,
that I may send thee away .
And Saul arose,

And they went out both of them ,
he and Samuel, abroad.
And as they were going down
to the end of the city ,
Samuel said to Saul,
bid the servant pass on before us ,
(and he passed on)

But stand thou still a while ,
That I may shew thee the word of God.

Question: With what ceremonial ritual
did Samuel make Saul King.

God says in: 1 Samuel 10 : 1 – 9

Then Samuel took a vial of oil ,
and poured it upon his head ,
and kissed him ,
and said ,
Is it not because the Lord hath anointed thee
to be Captain over his inheritance ?
When thou art departed from me today,
then thou shalt find two men by Rachel's sepulcher
in the border of Benjamin at Zelzah;
and they will say unto thee,
the asses which thou wentest to seek are found:
and, lo, thy father hath left the care of the asses ,
and sorroweth for you ,
saying,
what shall I do for my son?

Then shalt thou go on forward from thence,
and thou shalt come to the plain of Tabor,
and there shalt meet thee three men
going up to God to Bethel,
one carrying three kids,
and another carrying three loaves of bread,
and another carrying a bottle of wine :

And they will salute thee,
and give thee two loaves of bread ;
which thou shalt receive of their hands.
After that thou shalt come to the hill of God,
where is the garrison of the Philistines :

And it shall come to pass,

when thou art come thither to the city,
that thou shalt meet a company of prophets
coming down from the high place
with a psaltery,
and a tabret,
and a pipe,
and a harp,
before them;
and they shall prophesy:

And the Spirit of the Lord will come upon thee,
and thou shalt prophecy with them ,
and shalt be turned into another man.

And let it be,
when these signs are come unto thee,
that thou do as occasion serve thee;
for God is with thee.

And thou shalt go down before me to Gilgal;
And, behold ,
I will come down unto thee,
to offer burnt offerings
and to sacrifice
sacrifices of peace offerings .
Seven days shalt thou tarry,
till I come to thee ,
and show thee what thou shalt do.

And it was so ,
that when he had turned his back to go from Samuel,
God gave him another heart :
and all those signs came to pass that day.

Question: Did Samuel get a chance to present King Saul to the people of Israel ?

God says in: 1 Samuel 10 : 24 - 26

And Samuel said to all the people,
See ye him ,
whom the Lord hath chosen
That there is none like him
among all the people ?
And all the people shouted ,
God save the King .

Then Samuel told the people
the manner of the Kingdom,
and wrote it in a book,
And laid it up before the Lord.
And Samuel sent all the people away ,
every man to his house.

Question: Does God actually rule ,
even when there is a King in Power ?

God says in: Daniel 4 : 24 – 25

This is the interpretation, O King ,
and this is the decree of the most High,
which is come upon my Lord the King:
that they shall drive thee from men,
and thy dwelling shall be with the beasts of the field ,
and they shall make thee to eat grass as oxen ,
and they shall wet thee with the dew of heaven ,
and seven times shall pass over thee,
till thou know that the most High ruleth
in the Kingdom of men,
and
giveth it to whomsoever he will .

Authors Note: It is truly amazing to see how God worked
out this plan.
The Donkeys needed to be lost for Saul
and the servant to leave home to find Samuel.
The servant had to have brought that silver piece
to give to Samuel.
The Girls timing at the well ,
and them knowing the details of Samuels schedule.
And Samuel having been prepared by the Lord,
to know how to handle Saul .

It really does show how
God controls it all.

Question: Does God still control the whole earth ?

God says in: Psalm 24 : 1

> The earth is the Lord's
> and the fullness thereof ;
> The world,
> and they that dwell therein.

Question: If the earth belongs to God
and everyone that lives on earth,
does God actually control everything ,
even though all the nations
have their own King (or President) over them?

God says in: Psalms 47 : 2 – 8

> For the Lord most high is terrible ;
> he is a great King over all the earth.
>
> He shall subdue the people under us,
> and the nations under our feet .
>
> He shall choose our inheritance for us,
> the excellency of Jacob whom he loved. Selah.
>
> God is gone up with a shout ,
> The Lord with the sound of a trumpet.
> Sing praises to God ,
> sing praises :
> sing praises to our King,
> sing praises .
>
> For God is the King of all the earth :
> Sing ye praises with understanding .
>
> God reigneth over the heathen :
> God sitteth upon the throne of his holiness.

Authors Note: All over the world elected officials
are voting on whether
Euthanasia" is a good idea.

This should be a church problem .
Christians have a mandate to go out
and heal the sick
and tell them that the Kingdom of God
has come nigh unto them .
God never said :
" go out and kill those poor guys that have severe pain"!

In many countries ,
they are still voting
on whether killing unwanted babies
is a good idea.
God is always thinking about those little babies
in the mothers womb
and knows them all,
in great detail.

Question: How well does God know the little bablies in their mother womb ?

God says in: Psalms 139 : 13 - 18

> For thou hast possessed my reins :
> Thou hast covered me in my mother's womb.
> I will praise thee;
> for I am fearfully and wonderfully made:
> marvelous are thy works;
> and that my soul knoweth right well.
>
> My substance was not hid from thee,
> when I was made in secret,
> and curiously wrought
> in the lowest parts of the earth.
> Thine eyes did see my substance ,
> yet being unperfect;
> and in thy book all my members were written ,
> which in continuance were fashioned ,
> when as yet there was none of them.
> How precious also are thy thoughts unto me ,
> O God !
> How great is the sum of them !
> If I should count them ,
> they are more in number than the sand .

Authors comment:

Imagine,
God actually has every member,
of a little babies body written down
even before they are fully formed.

That would include the color of the eyes,
the shape of the ears,
the little nose,
the fingers and toes,
all of the organs,
and even the whispy hair color.

Governments are continually voting
on whether certain sins
should be considered alright now;
as if our God is flexible,
and not quite up to date
on our modern societies.

God is not democratic .

In the last 47 years,
Governments have been altering
the long standing laws ,
that were based on the Christian Bible.

In 1841 the Canadian Government criminalized
sexual relations between people of the same sex,
even if they were consensual,
and occurred in the privacy
of their home.
The criminal code imposed the death penalty
for this crime.

Then at the start of Canadian Confederation in 1867,
homosexuality was punishable under Canada's criminal
law by up to 14 years in prison.

In 1969, that law was amended
by the Pierre Trudeau government,
by decriminalizing acts of sodomy
between consenting adults
of at least 21 years of age.

Today they can legally marry and adopt children .

When I was young,
there were critical votes in parliaments,
as to whether stores should stay open on a Sunday.

Government officials reflected on
the fourth of the "ten commandments",
"remember the Sabbath Day to keep it Holy"
Exodus 20 : 8 - 11

I played on a city baseball team ,
and we played tournaments
against American teams
over a whole weekend,
and even on a Sunday.
But we couldn't host those teams in Canada
on a Sunday.

In Canada , each province and territory
had it's own legislation
regarding employment standards and Sunday shopping.

Much later, in 1982, the Supreme Court of Canada
upheld the Lord's Day Act.
However, at that time, only the Canadian Bill of Rights
existed.

That document only protected existing Canadian rights.
As a result, the Court noted
that Canada was an overwhelmingly Christian Country
that had accepted Sunday closing laws for years.
The Court determined that the Lords Day Act
did not force people to practice Christianity
or stop them practicing their own.

However ,
later that year ,
the Canadian Charter of Rights and Freedoms
was introduced,
ensuring freedom of conscience and religion,
regardless of existing Federal or Provincial laws.

On April 24,1985 the Supreme Court of Canada
ruled that the Lords Day Act
violated Canadians freedom of religion .

From the 1985 ruling, Canadian Parliament
again examined the original purpose of the act.
It found that the Christian value
of keeping Sunday holy,
had been incorporated into a law
that affected all Canadians, Christian or not .

This law, "the Lords Day Act",
prevented non Christians
from performing otherwise legal activities, on Sundays.
This was inconsistent with the Canadian Charter .

In my lifetime
people have come to believe
that God's commandments
are subject to change
by democratic vote.

God has never been democartic.

Chapter 20

Christians and Politics

The Doctrine of Christ
Ronald F. Peters

Question: In all cultures,
people tend to speak negatively
about their President
or about their Prime Minister
or about the King of their country .
What does God think about that ?

God says in: Exodus 22 : 28

Thou shalt not revile the Gods
(God and the Lord Jesus)
nor curse the ruler of thy people .

Question: Does that include anyone that rules over us ?

God says in: the Acts 23: 4 – 5

And they that stood by said ,
revilest thou God's High Priest ?
Then said Paul,
I wist not , Brethren ,
that he was the High Priest:
for it is written ,
thou shalt not speak evil
of the ruler of thy people.

Question: Why does God not want us
to speak evil of anyone?

God says in: St Mark 7 : 14-16

And when he had called all the people unto him ,
he said unto them ,
hearken unto me everyone of you,
and understand:
There is nothing from without a man ,
that entering into him can defile him ,
but
the things which come out of him,
those are they that defile the man .
If any man have ears to hear,
let him hear .

Question: So, if the evil things we speak , defile us ,
then does what we speak
have "reprocussions" ?

God says in: St. Mark 11 : 22 – 23

And Jesus answering saith unto them ,
Have faith in God
For verily I say unto you ,
That whosoever shall say unto this mountain,
Be thou removed,
and be thou cast into the sea;
and shall not doubt in his heart,
but shall believe that those things
which he saith
shall come to pass;
he shall have whatsoever he saith.

Question: If those things we say about our leaders
are believed in our hearts
and we believe those things ,
that we are saying about them ,
then are we merely reinforcing the bad things
that our leaders are doing,
and making things worse ?

God says in: Proverbs 20 : 2

The fear of a King
is as the roaring of a lion:
whoso provoketh him to anger
sinneth against his own soul .

Question: What kind of reprocussions can people expect, if they speak against their rulers?

God says in: 2 Peter 2: 9 – 13

The Lord knoweth how to deliver the godly
out of temptations
and to reserve the unjust unto the day of judgment
to be punished :

But chiefly them
that walk after the flesh
in the lust of uncleanness,
and despise government .

Presumptuous are they ,
selfwilled,
they are not afraid
to speak evil of dignities

Whereas angels ,
which are greater in power and might ,
bring not railing accusation
against them before the Lord.

But these ,
As natural brute beasts,
made to be taken and destroyed,
speak evil of the things that they understand not;
and shall utterly perish in their own corruption;

And shall receive the reward of unrighteousness,
as they that count it pleasure
to riot in the daytime.

Spots they are and blemishes,
sporting themselves with their own deceivings
while they feast with you.

Question: Does God still control the setting up of Kings like he did with King Saul and Samuel ?

God says in: Daniel 2 : 20 - 21

> Daniel answered and said,
> blessed be the name of God
> for ever and ever .
> for wisdom and might are his :
> and he changeth the times
> and the seasons :
>
> He removeth kings,
> and setteth up kings:
> He giveth wisdom unto the wise,
> and knowledge to them
> that know understanding .

Question: If God so obviously controls Kings does he also control what kind of King is on the throne?

God says in: Proverbs 21 : 1

> The Kings heart is in the hand of the Lord,
> as the rivers of water:
> he turneth it whithersoever he will.

Question: Does God also control what Kings think and the judgments they make ?

God says in: Proverbs 29 : 26

> Many seek the ruler's favour;
> but every man's judgment
> cometh from the Lord .

Question: Then is it really true that God is involved with the judgments in our courts ?

God says in: Proverbs 16 : 10

A divine sentence is in the lips of the King:
his mouth transgresseth not in judgment .

Question: If the people elect a King (or a President or a Prime Minister)
what should they be doing in order to have that King be a good ruler ?

God says in: 1 Samuel 12 : 13 – 15

Now therefore
behold the King whom ye have chosen,
and whom ye have desired !
and,
behold ,
the Lord hath set a King over you.

If
ye will
1) fear the Lord,
    and
2) serve him
    and
3) obey his voice
    and
4) not rebel

against the commandment of the Lord ,
then shall
both ye
and also the King that reigneth over you
continue following the Lord your God:

But
if ye will not obey the voice of the Lord,
but rebel against the commandment of the Lord,
then shall the hand of the Lord be against you,
as it was against your fathers.

Question: When God says,
Behold, the Lord hath set a King over you,
by what criteria does God determine
to set up an ungodly King,
or a righteous King,
and to build
and plant
a prosperous Kingdom
or to pluck up
and pull down
and destroy a kingdom?

God says in: Jeremiah 18 : 7 – 10

At what instant I shall speak
concerning a nation,
and concerning a Kingdom,
to pluck up,
and to pull down,
and to destroy it ;
If that nation,
against whom I have pronounced,
turn from their evil,
I will repent of the evil
that I thought to do unto them.
And
at what instant I shall speak
concerning a nation ,
and concerning a Kingdom,
to build and to plant it;
If it do evil in my sight,
that it obey not my voice,
then I will repent of the good,
wherewith I said I would benefit them.

Question: What if the people have not
obeyed the voice of the Lord
and their ruler has become a very bad one ?

God says in: 2 Chronicles 7 : 14

If my people,
which are called by my name ,
shall humble themselves,
and pray,
and seek my face,
and turn from their wicked ways ;
then
will I hear from heaven ,
and will forgive their sin,
and will heal their land.

Question: Does it help if we pray
for those that rule over us ?

God says in: 1 Timothy 2 : 1 – 3

I exhort therefore ,
that ,
first of all (these are the first things that
God expects when we pray),

supplications ,
prayers,
intercessions,
and giving of thanks,
be made for all men;

For Kings,
and for all that are in authority;

1. all men
2. for Kings (which in our case
    would be the President
    or Prime Minister
3. for all that are in authority,
    such as police , mayors,
    councilmen, Judges , teachers,
    premiers, govenors ,
    congressmen, and senators.
that we may lead a quiet and peaceable life
in all godliness and honesty.

For this is good and acceptable
in the sight of God our Saviour .

Question: How does God want us to respond to our rulers?

God says in: Romans 13 : 1 – 7

Let every soul
be subject unto higher powers.
For there is no power but of God:
the powers that be
are ordained of God.

Whosoever therefore resisteth the power,
resisteth the ordinance of God:
and they that resist
shall receive to themselves damnation.

For rulers
are not a terror
to good works,
but to the evil.

Wilt thou then not be afraid of the power?

Do that which is good,
and thou shalt have praise of the same :
For he is a minister of God to thee for good.
But
if thou do that which is evil,
be afraid ;
for he beareth not the sword in vain:
for he is the minister of God,
a revenger to execute wrath
upon him that doeth evil.

Wherefore
ye must needs be subject,
not only for wrath,
but also for conscience sake.

For this cause pay ye tribute also:
for they are God's ministers ,
attending continually upon this very thing.

Render therefore to all their dues:
tribute to whom tribute is due;
custom to whom custom ;
fear to whom fear ;
honour to whom honour.

Questions to God
There are four volumes .
Please note their content outline.

※ ※ ※

Questions to God , Volume 1
The Mystery of Life After Death – by Ronald F. Peters

Every persons current body will die.
We just don't know exactly when we are leaving.
So, where do people go right after they die ?
What is it like in the next world ?
What do we need to do,
to have a really super life in the other world ?
Some ecologists, scientists and theologians believe that the earth
is beginning to expire and that humans will need to leave this world,
possibly in this century.
The Bible tells us exactly how it is going to end .
Everyone is going to live many trillions of years, after we leave.
The time we spend in our current container,
is preparation time for the next world.
How are we to prepare,
to live in our new Spirit bodies ?
This is a fascinating book. It is perfect for Christian Bible Studies.
The entire book is written in "Question and Answer" format .

Questions to God, Volume 2
The actual doctrine of King Jesus – by Ronald F. Peters

The Christian Holy Bible says
there are two baptisms.
Nicodemus was told in St. John 3 : 5
" except a man be born of water
and of the Spirit,
he cannot enter into the Kingdom of God.
There is water baptism,
and the baptism of the Holy Spirit.
What makes them both very important ?
God made two contracts with earth people,
called covenants.
What has changed in the second contract ?
These contracts are only valid and legal,
if they are officially accepted.
Today, we accept contracts with an official signature.
The first contract was accepted by circumcision.
If a male wasn't circumcised,
he did not have a valid contract with God.
How is the second covenant to be accepted and validated ?
When King Jesus left planet earth ,
and knowing that he was leaving for many centuries,
what five things did he instruct us to do ?
Is God flexible, and is he democratic ?
How does God want us to be involved with politics ?
You'll be amazed at what God actually says.

Questions to God, Volume 3
How to hear the Voice of King Jesus – by Ronald F. Peters

Communicating with God is what God created us for.

Deuteronomy 28 : 1 – 2
And it shall come to pass,
if thou shalt hearken diligently (it means you need to listen really hard)
unto the voice of the Lord thy God,
to observe
and to do
all his commandments (whatever he tells you to do - you're his servant)
which I command thee this day,
that the Lord thy God will set thee on high
above all nations of the earth.

King Jesus said : St. John 10 : 27
My sheep hear my voice
and I know them
and they follow me. (following means,
you go places you didn't expect to go)
And yet ,
most Christians around the world have no idea,
how to hear the voice of King Jesus.

King Jesus said: St. John 18 : 37
Everyone that is of the truth,
heareth my voice.
To be in servant mode,
requires that one must be able to hear his voice
and then follow His Majesty , King Jesus,
wherever he leads you.
This book will show you how.

Questions to God - Volume 4
Messed Up Families – by Ronald F. Peters

All over the world marriages are failing.
Divorces in the USA :
There are 2.4 million marriages per year in the USA
There are 1.2 million divorces per year in the USA
First marriages fail 40 - 50 %
Second marriages fail 60 - 67 %

Abortions in the USA :
21% of all USA pregnancies end in abortion
2014 - 974,000 abortions
2013 - 983,000 abortions
2012 - 1.02 million abortions
2008 - 1.21 million abortions
1996 - 1.36 million abortions

Children from Fatherless homes
account for :
63 percent of suicides
73 percent of pregnant teenagers
90 percent of homeless and runaway children
70 percent of institutionalized juveniles
85 percent of behavioural disorders
80 percent of rapists
71 percent of all high school dropouts
75 percent of adolescent parents in chemical abuse centers
85 percent of youths in prison

Welfare homes - in 2012
- 309,467,000 people in the U.S.A.
- 109,631,000 living in households
taking federal welfare benefits = 35.4 percent

___

When people reject God, and refuse to live by his laws, trouble sets into their lives.
This book will show, how God intended for families to live.